HISTORIC HENRY COUNTY

An Illustrated History

By Michael Reaves

Published by the Henry County Chamber of Commerce

Historical Publishing Network
A division of Lammert Incorporated
San Antonio, Texas

Main Street McDonough in the mid-twentieth century.

PHOTO BY CHRISTINE PARK HANKINSON. COURTESY
OF THE HENRY COUNTY GENEALOGICAL SOCIETY.

First Edition

Copyright © 2004 Historical Publishing Network

ISBN: 1-893619-38-9

Library of Congress Card Catalog Number: 2004100127

Historic Henry County: An Illustrated History

author:	Michael Reaves
editor:	Gene Morris, Jr.
contributing writer for "Sharing the Heritage":	Eric Dabney

Historical Publishing Network

president:	Ron Lammert
vice president:	Barry Black
project manager:	Lou Ann Murphy
director of operations:	Charles A. Newton III
administration:	Angela Lake
	Donna M. Mata
	Judi Free
book sales:	Dee Steidle
graphic production:	Colin Hart
	Michael Reaves

PRINTED IN CANADA

The dam at Miller's Mill.
PHOTO BY RON & ALICE LEWIS. COURTESY OF
THE HENRY COUNTY GENEALOGICAL SOCIETY.

CONTENTS

INTRODUCTION

Welcome to *HISTORIC HENRY COUNTY*. This book is written to help the reader gain a brief understanding of the history of Henry County from primarily an economic perspective. In history, as with any subject, there are many ways to approach and present a great mass of material to an audience. The way that I have used to analyze the history of Henry County is in no way the "best" or the "worst" way to approach the history of Henry County. This history is simply one perspective on the large subject of the county's history. With this in mind, I would be remiss in not recommending to the reader two additional readings from Henry County historians that have approached the subject with different methodologies.

The first book I would recommend to someone wanting to know about Henry County history is, official Henry County Historian Gene Morris Jr.'s *True Southerners: A Pictorial History of Henry County*. In *True Southerners*, Morris uses the records of normal citizens to give the reader a real sense of daily life in the different periods of Henry County's history. If you are interested in social history and want to emotionally connect to the people of past then this well-written, professionally produced, and beautifully illustrated book is for you.

If you had ancestors in Henry County or are interested in genealogy, then Joseph Henry Hightower Moore's *First Families of Henry County, Georgia*, will answer all your questions. This massive 766-page tome has comprehensive genealogical data along with family histories of just about everyone who ever passed through Henry County. This book is a labor of love and will be an essential reference for anyone looking into Henry County's past.

First Families can be purchased at the Genealogical Society of Henry & Clayton Counties' headquarters at 71 Macon Street in McDonough and *True Southerners* is available at Moye's Pharmacy in McDonough. In addition to these two books, the society has dozens of other books on Henry County's history for purchase and a large library of books, newspaper records, and microfilm records that pertain to all facets of Henry County and Georgia history. The society is the premier repository for historical sources in Henry County and one can expect to find at least one or two of Henry County's premier historians to be at the society at any given time. Whether you are starting an intense research project or just want to make an interesting day trip, the society is well worth your time.

I hope that this book, along with the other previously mentioned and highly recommended readings, helps give a better understanding of the triumphs and tragedies of the people of Henry County and inspires the latest generation of Henry County residents to look into and appreciate the rich history of Henry County.

Michael Reaves
December 2003

CHAPTER I

THE LAND BEFORE HENRY COUNTY

The land that would later become Henry County has a proud history that predates European settlement. Located in the fertile Piedmont Plateau, the land's natural resources attracted and provided a bountiful and idyllic existence for the Creek Indians and their predecessors for almost a millennia. These same bucolic lands would also attract American settlers who would seal the fate of the Creeks.

Etowah Indian Mounds State Historic Site, Cartersville, Georgia.
COURTESY OF THE GEORGIA DEPARTMENT OF INDUSTRY, TRADE & TOURISM.

THE FIRST PEOPLE

The Creeks Indians were the dominate Native American group in what would be central and southern regions of Georgia and Alabama; but they were not the first group to settle in the area. The mysterious civilization of the Mound Builders predated the Creeks by at least five hundred years. Archeologists and anthropologists know little about this civilization but what is known is impressive. The Mound Builders inhabited Georgia from approximately 800 to 1200 A.D. They built large earth mounds temples, towns, and stone fortifications. The most famous examples of these are the Ocmulgee Fields near Macon; Etowah Mounds near Cartersville; and the remains of a large Mound Builder fortress at Fort Mountain near Chatsworth, Georgia. In Henry County the remains of a Mound Builder fort are located near the Indian Creek Reservoir. It is believed, based on their engineering skill, size and number of their settlements, and recovered artifacts, that the Mound Builders were much more advanced civilization and had a larger population than any of the Indian civilizations that came after them. One of the biggest questions about the Mound Builders concerns what led to the demise of this advance civilization. According to Creek legend, when they emigrated from their original homes in the Southern Rockies, around 1000 to 1200 A.D., the Mound Builders were already gone and their structures were as much an enigma to Creeks as they were to later Georgian settlers. Some anthropologists theorize that the Mound Builder civilization may have been critically weakened by war or disease may have been introduced by the incoming Creek tribes, but this is simply the best theory and no general consensus has been reached on what happened to the first civilization that inhabited what would be the future Henry County.

THE CREEKS

Unlike the Mound Builders, the Creek Indians are much better known to history and

had a vibrant society before they were removed to Oklahoma in the 1820s. The Creek Indians were a group of ethnically diverse tribes that had been united by shared social structures and political alliances. The name Creek came from English traders in seventeenth century Georgia and the Carolinas. In times past, the Creeks would usually identify to themselves by which Creek town or clan they were from. Many modern Creeks refer to themselves as Muskogee, from the Algonquin word meaning "people of the wetlands," but this term is confusing. The Muskogee were the dominant Creek tribe and language, but the Creeks had other tribes, most notably, the Alabama, Koasati, Natchez, Hitchiti, Chickasaw, Shawnee, Yuchi, and Yamasee; and the languages of Alabama, Koasiti, Hitchiti, Natchez, Yuchi, and Shawnee were also used in the Creek Confederacy. For clarity sake, modern anthropologists and ethnographers use the Muskogee name only when referring to those specific Creek tribes that were Muskogee and use Creek in reference to the whole civilization.

Etowah Indian Mounds in Cartersville.
COURTESY OF THE GEORGIA DEPARTMENT OF INDUSTRY, TRADE & TOURISM.

SE-LOC-TA,
A CREEK CHIEF.

PUBLISHED BY F. W. GREENOUGH, PHILAD.ᵃ

*A 1836 lithograph of the Creek
Chief Se-loc-ta.*

Traditional Creek life was centered on the local village unit. A Creek village, commonly referred to as *talwa*, consisted of approximately two dozen houses radiating out from a center square. The center square was the ceremonial and governmental center of the village. On any given day, one could expect to find the village headman/wise man, the *micos*, along with the chief warrior, the *tastanage*, in the village square discussing matters with any warriors that were not out in the wilderness actively hunting game. When warriors were not in the village square they were often out hunting for deer, buffalo, bear, or wild turkey. The game gathered during hunts was supplemented by corn, beans, squash, and potatoes raised by the women of the tribe.

When not taking care of the drudgeries of day-to-day existence, the Creeks kept busy with sports. The sports had the dual function of training young warriors in quasi-combat situations and they provided a "friendly" way for tribes to settle disputes before they led to open warfare. The Creeks had two main games that

they would play: Chunkey and the ball game. In Chunkey, players would roll a stone disk into a field then attempt to throw their spear closest to the stone disk.

The other game, simply known as the ball game, was similar to an extremely violent game of rugby. There would be two teams of players whose goal was to get a leather ball down the game field to the opponent's goal. The catch with ball game was that the teams could use any means necessary to get the ball where they wanted. This lack of rules led to frequent permanent injuries or death, especially when the teams were from opposing tribes.

When disputes could not by solved by games, then war often came about. It is important to note that the Creek way of war, as with many other Native American tribes, was highly ritualistic and very different from contemporary European warfare or modern warfare. Before any hostile action was taken, both tribes would enact ritual ceremonies to announce the start of hostilities. When a tribe went to war against another tribe the goal was to slay and scalp a handful of warriors from the enemy's camp and get back to one's own village. After a number of scalping raids by both sides, the headman and chief warriors from each tribe would get together and compare their scalp counts. The one with the least amount of scalps

would be declared the loser and usually acquiesce to the usually minor and ceremonial terms of the winning tribe. Rarely did warfare go to point that one tribe was driven off their land or wiped out. This type of piecemeal warfare that kept Creek society together for hundreds of years would prove ineffective and counter-productive when they encountered Europeans.

THE REMOVAL OF THE CREEKS

The Creeks Confederacy, which consisted of the Lower Creeks of Georgia and the Carolinas and the Upper Creeks of Alabama, had used sophisticated diplomatic maneuvering between opposing European colonial powers in order to secure the Creek lands. This strategy served Creek interests well for the better part of two centuries. The British, Spanish, and French were played one against another with the Creeks never totally siding with one faction or another.

Unfortunately for the Creeks, as the political situation changed in North America, they failed to change their diplomatic strategy and this lack of foresight led directly to the Creeks removal to Oklahoma. There were factors that changed the political landscape for the Creeks: first, the American Revolution; second, the Napoleonic

Wars and the corresponding removal of most European interests from the North American Continent; and finally, the penetration of American settlers into the Upper Creek lands in Alabama. All three of these situations were misunderstood by most Creek leaders and their bad decisions, combined with the growing State of Georgia, would be fatal for the Creek Confederacy.

The American Revolution was an unexpected political shift for the Creeks and they reacted by choosing the wrong side. The Creeks decided to throw their support to the British and, even though hindsight shows that it was a bad choice, at the time the choice would have seemed to be the wisest by far. The common political wisdom of the time, in both North America and Europe, concerning the American Revolution came to the conclusion that it was a foolish endeavor and the British would make quick work of the rebels. The British were the premier naval force at the time and had a substantial standing army in North America. At that period, the British did not have any particular worries about major French or Spanish interference in the American Revolution. Finally, and most importantly for the Creeks, the colonies with which they had the most contact—Georgia and the Carolinas—were very loyal to Britain and were not subject to anywhere near the level of rebel activity of the northern colonies. When the British withdrew from North America, the Creeks were surprised to learn that they sided with the wrong people and were faced with a new American federal government that was not fond of them and a state government, Georgia, that was actively out to get them. Things would only get worse for the Creeks in the following years.

The dawn of the nineteenth century only brought more problems for the Creeks. The consequences of the Napoleonic Wars in Europe would reverberate ominously for the Creeks. As Napoleon roamed around continental Europe, carving up the old regimes with abandon, he was faced with the problem of financing the maintenance of huge armies in the field. One of the many solutions he came up with was to sell French interests in North America to the United States in what was famously known as the Louisiana Purchase in

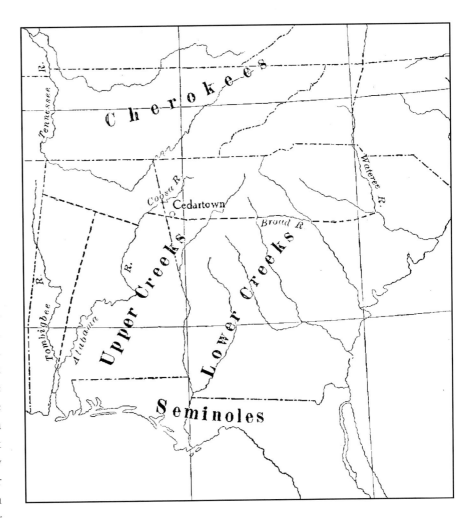

1803. This was followed by the abandonment of Florida by French-controlled Spain in 1821. These political changes were a shock for the Creeks who had for two centuries maintained their security on the premise of playing one European power against another.

The Creek Confederacy was further weakened by a political split between the Upper Creek tribes of Alabama and the Lower Creeks tribes of Georgia over the issue of whether or not to cooperate with the United States. The Lower Creeks had been in contact with European settlers for much longer than the Upper Creeks. They were used to trading, interacting, and negotiating with Europeans and consequently had a much more realistic assessment of the Creek Confederacy's strengths and weaknesses in comparison with the newly created United States. The Upper Creeks had been relatively isolated from European settlers by their location far away from the eastern seaboard. The isolation of the Upper Creeks ended early of the nineteenth century when the United States' population started to

A map of the Indian Territories.

FROM *HISTORY OF GEORGIA* BY ROBERT BROOKS.

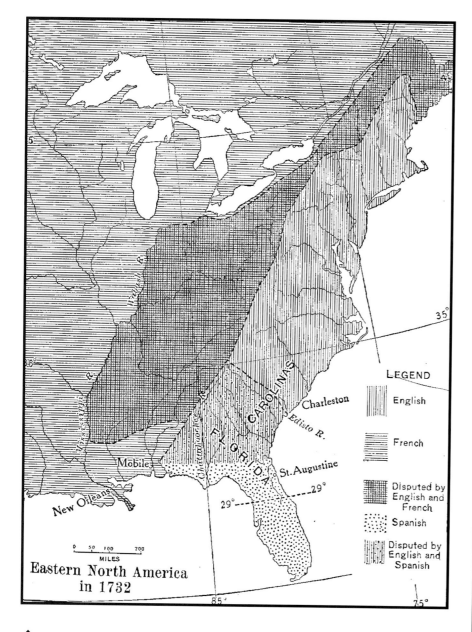

LEGEND

||| English

≡ French

▦ Disputed by English and French

⋰ Spanish

▥ Disputed by English and Spanish

Eastern North America
in 1732

Above: A map illustrating the different political spheres of influence that surrounded the Creeks.

FROM *HISTORY OF GEORGIA* BY ROBERT BROOKS.

Right: A finalized version of the Treaty of Indian Springs that made it into the Congressional Record.

COURTESY OF THE LIBRARY OF CONGRESS.

First, the Lower Creeks realized they could not militarily compete with the military power of the United States. Second, they believed the federal government would protect the Creeks from the encroachment by the State of Georgia. This policy of appeasing the federal government worked until the administration of President James Monroe in 1816. Monroe, influenced by the council of Andrew Jackson and John C. Calhoun, was sympathetic to the State of Georgia's desire for Creek lands and, in a series of treaties from 1818 to 1825, the lower Creeks were voluntarily removed from Georgia. The Treaty of Indian Springs in 1821, negotiated by McIntosh, gave Georgia the land that became Henry County. McIntosh was killed in 1824 by a group of Upper Creeks from Alabama, who resisted the encroachment of the United States into traditional Creek land. Less than a decade after the Treaty of Indian Springs and the founding of Henry County all the Creeks were removed from Georgia and Alabama and moved into Oklahoma.

geometrically increase and moved west into the frontier of the Ohio and Mississippi Valleys. The Upper Creeks reacted violently to the encroachment of American squatters on their land. In the first major political split within the Creek Nation, the Upper Creeks sided with the British during the War of 1812 and following the exhortations of Tecumseh, carried on the conflict until 1814, long after the British had left North America, in what would be called the Creek War. The Lower Creeks sided with the American government in both the War of 1812 and the Creek War but the damage had been done.

The Lower Creeks, led by William McIntosh, a resident of Indian Springs, in what would later become Henry County, tried to work with the United States government for two main reasons.

CHAPTER II

ANTEBELLUM HENRY COUNTY

The cyclical movements of Americans ever westward in the early nineteenth century had a profound impact upon Henry County. Henry County was founded and quickly prospered as part of the first great expansion west of the American frontier; but almost as quickly as it was founded, the continuing expansion of the American frontier created a series of circumstances that led to the decline of Henry County before the Civil War.

THE FOUNDING OF HENRY COUNTY

Henry County was created on May 15, 1821, by the Georgia State Assembly in an act that simultaneously established the Dooly, Houston, Monroe, Fayette, and Henry Counties from the Creek lands obtained by the Treaty of Indian Springs that had been signed earlier that year. Henry County was much larger in its inception than it is today. As originally laid out, Henry County was almost eighty square miles, three times its current size, and contained all or portions of the present-day counties of Fulton, DeKalb, Rockdale, Newton, Butts, Spalding, Fayette, and Clayton. The original boundaries of Henry County did not last long. Almost instantly, in political time, sections of Henry County were carved out to create new counties. On Christmas Eve in 1821, the General Assembly created Fayette and Newton Counties out of Henry County. Almost a year later, on December 9, 1822, DeKalb was created from Henry County. In 1825, Henry County land was used to form part of the new county of Butts.

The Hampton Railroad Depot today has been converted to city offices and a museum.

These early partitions of Henry County came from the normal process of settling and organizing a frontier land. As more people settled in Henry County, it became necessary for the size of the county to be split up for administrative purposes. In the early nineteenth century, old Indian paths and unimproved dirt roads were the normal means of overland transportation. Twenty miles would be the normal distance that anyone would safely expect to travel during a full-day trip. To go any faster, even on horseback, invited disaster by tripping over hazards in the dirt roads that were created anew with every heavy rain. This logistical constraint from the roads meant that county officials could only reasonably administer what they could reach in a day or less. The representatives of the General Assembly carved smaller counties out of Henry County on this idea that good governance was most likely occur if officials could reach anywhere in their county within a day's ride.

The later partitions of Henry County were done for more political than logistical purposes. In the period of 1830-1870, Henry County was economically weaker than its neighbors and carried less weight in Georgia state politics. These disadvantages allowed ambitious politicians in neighboring counties to carve away parts of Henry County in order to enrich their own counties or to create brand new political fiefdoms. In 1850, Butts County took more of Henry County and five more times,

until 1875, the Butts County line advanced deeper into Henry County. In 1851, Spalding County gobbled up some of southwest Henry County. In 1858, for political reasons, Clayton County was created from Henry County. The final county to be carved out of Henry County occurred in 1870 when Rockdale was created. In less than fifty years Henry County had been created and in turn gave birth to seven counties. It was from this generously given land that Henry County acquired the proud moniker, "The Mother of Counties."

THE FIRST SETTLERS OF HENRY COUNTY

The first settlers into Henry County were brave frontier settlers in the best tradition of the American frontier. They were rugged individualists who were seeking new lives for themselves and their families and were taking the risk of coming into unknown country to make a living off of land unfamiliar to them.

Even before Henry County had been officially formed they had started settling within the future bounds of the county and, by 1822, new settlers were pouring into Henry County. Many of the early settlers of Henry County were brought by the 1821 land lottery, where a person could draw for one to two plots of land. Each plot was 202.5 acres in size. The settlers initially made their way into Henry County along old Indian trading paths from Augusta, Georgia. The Creek Indians had used most of the land that would be Henry County as hunting grounds; consequently, when settlers arrived in the early 1820s they found almost completely virgin wilderness.

The virgin condition of the soil was very important for the first settlers of Henry County. In 1820, agricultural practices did not include the best understanding of field rotation and fertilization practices that would, later in the late nineteenth century, regenerate the nutrients and restore the productivity of fallow fields. Therefore, there was the general belief that once farmland was exhausted it was better to start a new farm on virgin land rather than wait for years for fields to become productive again. This belief was one of the factors that drove the American frontier west during the nineteenth century.

Immigrants from other states and foreign countries were Henry County's initial pioneers. The settlers from other states were from the generation that fought in the American Revolution and their immediate children. Some of the older settlers were veterans of the Revolutionary War. Many younger setters had fought in the War of 1812 or one of the various Indian brush wars that flared up in the late-eighteenth and early nineteenth centuries. The immigrants to Henry County from foreign countries came mostly from the impoverished sections of Western Europe. Many refugees from the hopelessness of Ireland, economic malaise of Scotland, and political uncertainties in the states that would later become Germany came directly from their homelands to Henry County.

THE BOOM & BUST OF ANTEBELLUM HENRY COUNTY

McDonough was the first town established in Henry County and it was a boomtown. Early in 1822 the Georgia State Assembly appointed commissioners to set up government for Henry County. One of the duties of the commissioners was to find a site for the county seat. On April 15, 1823, they bought two hundred acres on which to establish a county seat and subdivide into town lots for sale to the general public. This led to, on December 17, 1823, just before Henry

County's second birthday, the village of McDonough being incorporated as the county seat for Henry County. McDonough was named for Commodore Thomas MacDonough, who, in a naval battle defeated the British at the Battle of Plattsburgh during the War of 1812.

Many of the people who came to settle in the new town of McDonough in the mid- to late-1820s were different from the initial wave of yeoman farmers that had settled in rural Henry County. The people settling in McDonough were hoping that it would be the next big boomtown that would make fortunes for those satisfying

Above: The Shingleroof Campground as it appears today.

Below: The pulpit of Shingleroof Campground.

the needs of rural Georgians. Merchants came hoping to act as the middlemen for farmers wanting to get their products to market further east. Agents appeared representing East Coast manufacturers and importers who wanted to sell their merchandize to rural farmers. Professionals, such as doctors, lawyers, and accountants also came hoping to fill the need for their services in what they hoped would soon be a thriving metropolis. By 1828, according to the *Gazetteer of the State of Georgia*, McDonough had 8 stores, 7 mechanical shops, 4 doctors, 3 law offices, an academy, two churches, and a new courthouse. All these stores were not for

the paltry forty-six residential houses of McDonough; rather they were built to service the much larger number of rural customers and potential customers that had yet to move to Henry County.

In spite of all the high hopes of the McDonough residents, the growing pains stemming from being a boomtown would almost destroy McDonough as quickly as it had been created. There were three factors that would hurt McDonough in the 1830s and 1840s: the economics of the railroad, cotton production, and the continued expansion of the American Frontier. The first blow to McDonough came in 1833, when the first railroad went through Madison and ended in the small and somewhat insignificant village of Marthasville. The railroad going through Marthasville almost instantly turned the sleepy village into the city of Atlanta and the commercial center for the antebellum South. More insult to injury came when the railroad extensions from Atlanta went around Henry County on both the east and the west. The new towns of Griffin and Jonesboro sprung up along the railroad and prospered. Many of the people who had set up shop in McDonough left for greener fields in these rail towns. By 1845 the exodus of people from McDonough left it in a state of suspended animation and, in 1850, the power in Henry County shifted to the new town of Bear Creek (later renamed Hampton) that

sprung up on the small corner where the railroad passed through Henry County.

The urban exodus from McDonough was accompanied by a rural exodus of farmers from Henry County. In antebellum Georgia, cotton was king and Henry County lay in the agricultural belt of Georgia most hospitable to cotton. While abundant cotton production is good for the larger farmers, cotton production was quite unfavorable for the smaller farmer. First and foremost, for cotton production to be economically viable, one had to produce enough to afford the shipping costs to the eastern ports where it would fetch the best prices from European traders. The small farmer couldn't produce enough cotton to cover the freight costs east. Also, the harvesting of cotton itself was a problem in that it was very labor intensive and

tended to quickly drain the soil of its resources. Many times the smaller farmers could not afford the slaves or hired hands needed to cultivate a large area of cotton. In addition, when a couple seasons of cotton production had worn down the fields, a small farmer did not have enough land to allow for crop rotation among fields and did not have the available money to buy additional fields. All these economic factors that discouraged the small farmer worked in favor of the plantations. The larger farms and plantations could cultivate enough cotton to make it profitable, had enough slaves, and could afford to buy up the lands of smaller farmers who had given up and moved west.

❖

Above: A cabin from the Shingleroof Campground.

Bottom, left: One of Henry County's original homes. This log cabin was built in 1842 by Turner Hunt Clements. The cabin has recently been moved to Heritage Park in McDonough.

Bottom, right: The remains of Miller's Mill.

Many of the poorest farmers in Henry County chose to move to new lands opening in the west. Just as the initial frontier status of Henry County in the 1820s brought many people looking for a better life many of the same people chose in the 1840s and 1850s to again pick up their families and move west for fresh opportunity in the expansion of the American frontier. By the eve of the Civil War, Henry County was rich on paper, with a real estate value of over $1.7 million and a personal property value of over $2.8 million, but this prosperity was disproportionally weighted toward the rich farming class. What middle-class professionals Henry County had in earlier years had been attracted to Atlanta or the surrounding rail towns and many of the poorer farmers left the state altogether. With the exception of the plantation class, most of the people who stayed in Henry County lived a life of hard-scrabble subsistence farming where they grew just enough to feed themselves and, if lucky, sold what extra crop they had for a few dollars to help with the essentials. Unfortunately, for the hardy souls, both rich and poor, who stayed in Henry County through the 1850s, the next two decades would bring the hardest years every faced by the people of the county.

CHAPTER III

HENRY COUNTY DURING THE
CIVIL WAR AND RECONSTRUCTION

The Civil War and Reconstruction were some of the most difficult years for the people of Henry County. Even though most Henry Countians had initially opposed the secession of Georgia from the Union, they faithfully stood with their state when Georgia voted to secede and contributed more than their fair share of soldiers to the Confederate War effort. Both those who put on the Confederate uniform and those who remained at home felt the full consequences of the Civil War. Soldiers from Henry County served with distinction in most of the major battles of the Civil War. On the home front, the people left behind first suffered indirectly from the economic deprivations of a war-time economy and were later directly devastated by Sherman's infamous March to the Sea. Henry County's indignities did not end with the end of the war. During Reconstruction, the Confederate veterans came back to Henry County to find their lands ravaged and had to rebuild with little to no help from the state or federal government. This period from 1860 to 1874 was easily the bleakest in Henry County's history.

The Confederate Memorial in McDonough, Georgia.

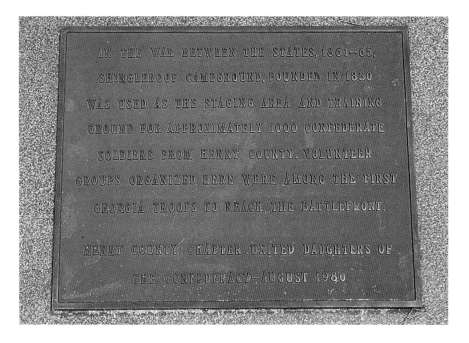

❖

Above: The Confederate Placard at Shingleroof Campground. The campground was used as a mustering site during the Civil War.

Below: A historic Georgia flag located at the Locust Grove Institute Museum.

HENRY COUNTY'S REACTION TO THE START OF THE CIVIL WAR

The people of Henry County were against Georgia's secession from the Union. They indicated as much by sending anti-secessionist delegates to the special session of the Georgia legislature that eventually voted to secede. Even though the populace was initially against secession it would be a mistake to assume that Henry County did not carry its weight during the war. The people of Henry County, very much like most people of that period in the United States, did not think of themselves as Americans. Instead they thought themselves as citizens of their state. Their first political loyalties were to their state.

The notion of state supremacy and a historically weak and unobtrusive federal government was the reason that, when Georgia threw her lot in with her sister states in the South, the people of Henry County responded with absolute support for the Confederacy.

The best measure of how wholeheartedly Henry County supported the Confederacy is by examining the huge proportion of Henry County's free male population that enlisted and fought in the Civil War. By 1862, the first full year of the conflict, Henry County had already produced over one thousand men for Confederate forces. This was over one-fifth of the free male population of Henry County. Henry County produced the Company G, Nineteenth Georgia Infantry; Company H, "Zachary's Rangers," of the Twenty-seventh Georgia Infantry; Company K, Twenty-second Georgia Infantry; Company A, Fourth-fourth Regiment of the Army of Northern Virginia; Company F, the "Dixie Guards," Fifty-third Regiment of the Army of Northern Virginia; and Company B, Thirtieth Georgia Regiment of the Army of Northern Virginia. Company K of the Twenty-second Georgia Infantry, which served through the entire war, lost seventy percent of its men at Gettysburg. The Twenty-second is a typical example of the hardships and mettle displayed by Henry County units in the Civil War.

THE HOME FRONT

The civilians left behind in Henry County suffered greatly as the war dragged on. Very early in the war, the Union had effectively blockaded most Confederate ports. This blockade had the immediate and devastating effect of cutting the South off from large-scale European trade and had a devastating effect on the Southern economy. Without regular revenue from cotton, the farmers of Henry County were forced to go into large-scale subsistence farming. While hardly as profitable as cotton, the foodstuffs that were grown within Henry County and other central Georgia counties were essential for the Confederate war effort. There is an old military saying that goes, "Strategy is for amateurs, logistics is for professionals." This maxim indicates the harsh military truth that it is often much harder to keep an army fed and

clothed than it is to fight a battle. Henry County lies in the middle of what was the breadbasket of the confederacy. In the more northerly Confederate States, there were constant movements of armies that devastated and exhausted the agricultural capacity of those states. Whereas, central Georgia, which had been spared major military engagements until the summer of 1864, was able to produce a steady and much needed supply of food to the armies operating in Tennessee and Virginia.

Unfortunately, the relative tranquility of Henry County was to be shattered in July 1864 when the war came to Atlanta. On May 7, 1884, General William Tecumseh Sherman started his advance toward Atlanta from Chickamauga. The brilliant and capable Confederate General Joseph E. Johnson, was forced to make a fighting retreat toward Atlanta due to the overwhelming number of Union troops—over 98,000—facing his army of 50,000. During his retreat to Atlanta, Johnson fought well and resourcefully with the idea of drawing Sherman into a prolonged siege of Atlanta that Sherman would have difficulty maintaining so deep in the Confederacy. Upon reaching Atlanta, Sherman was forced into siege warfare of the city and consigned to a number of raids around the perimeter of Atlanta. On July 22, Sherman sent a cavalry group commanded by

General Judson Kilpatrick to seize provisions in Henry County. That night, Kilpatrick's men came into McDonough, seized the commissary stores at McDonough and, out of spite, destroyed a portion of the county records in the old county courthouse. These raiders were successfully driven out of Henry County by Generals Lawrence Ross and Samuel Ferguson who forced the Union cavalry into a retreat at Cotton Indian River at Peachstone Shoals Road. The hasty retreat by Kilpatrick and his men resulted in their losing horses and wagons and cancelled out any benefit received by raiding McDonough.

After Johnson had successfully brought his army to Atlanta and was successfully holding off Sherman from the city, President Jefferson Davis sealed the fate of Atlanta and the Confederacy over petty politics. Davis had never liked Johnson and used the situation in Atlanta to replace him. Johnson, one of the best generals of the Confederacy, was replaced with one of its least competent and humble generals, John B. Hood. Hood, who had dreams of glory, believed in the offensive even when it was the wrong tactic to take. Sherman, knowing Hood's temperament and judgment, managed to entice him out of Atlanta, in a series of battles that ended with the Battle of Jonesboro on September 1, 1864. Sherman seized the city with little trouble on September 2. This was a fatal and unexpected blow for the South and the miracle that enabled Lincoln to be elected for a second term. This Confederate defeat would

Above: General Joseph E. Johnson
COURTESY OF THE LIBRARY OF CONGRESS.

Below: A Civil War-era cannon in front of Locust Grove City Hall (the old Locust Grove Institute building).

Civil War reenactors.

COURTESY OF THE GEORGIA DEPARTMENT OF
INDUSTRY, TRADE & TOURISM.

soon bring Union punishment that would devastate Henry County, along with much of Georgia, and shock the whole world in its brutality and effectiveness.

SHERMAN'S MARCH THROUGH HENRY COUNTY

With the Union forces camped in Atlanta, Sherman faced a problem. He had Hood's army on the loose, heading north, threatening to cut off his lines of communications and supply routes to the Union. If he protected his lines of supply and chased Hood north, then it would cancel out much of the benefit of the Atlanta campaign. Sherman, who had a better understanding of contemporary warfare than many of his fellow generals, realized that the fertile counties of Georgia were as important to the Confederate war effort as any army in the field. He therefore decided to make a novel expedition in which he took what his army needed from the agricultural and industrial infrastructure of Georgia. Sherman's March to the Sea was the first hint of the concept of "Total War," which was to come to full fruition during the Second World War, in which civilian infrastructure is considered a legitimate military target. Sherman's cold calculation and the average soldiers pent-up frustration and desire for revenge combined to make the March to the Sea one of the most infamous acts of the nineteenth century.

McDonough, while suffering greatly in the March to the Sea, did not endure the total devastation of some other Georgia cities. There are two reasons that McDonough was spared the worse of Sherman: first, the efforts of Dr. Lewis M. Tye, and second, timing. Dr. Tye, one of the more beloved of Henry County's historical figures, was from North Carolina and moved to McDonough in 1838. After receiving his medical education in Augusta, he came back to McDonough and opened up his medical practice. During the Civil War he was a surgeon

for the Fourth Regiment, Georgia State Troops. When Sherman came to McDonough, Dr. Tye diligently worked on the Northern soldiers and managed to secure the safety of McDonough, with only one building being burned. According to local legend, Dr. Tye personally told the Union commander that he didn't like working with smoke in his eyes and this was enough to lighten the Union's hand in McDonough. A number of houses and stores were looted in McDonough, but only one house was burned and a local Baptist church was desecrated. This damage was light compared with the situation in Bear Creek (Hampton) were the whole town was burned to the ground by Union troops.

The second factor that saved Henry County from more widespread destruction was that Sherman's march had barely begun when it passed though Henry County. The soldiers in Henry County were still in their normal marching formation and had not yet dispersed into the wide columns that served to obliterate many other parts of Georgia; however, destructive foraging parties raided farms, mills, and homes throughout the county.

As Sherman's forces left McDonough, they started their march in earnest with the destruction of two churches and a number of mills on their way out of the county. They also raided local farms, liberating any slaves they found and taking everything that was not nailed to the ground. It was this destruction of agricultural capital,

combined with the earlier raids in July and August on Henry County's food stores by both Union and Confederate forces, which would make lives much harder for the residents and returning veterans who would be trying to rebuild their lives during the Reconstruction years.

RECONSTRUCTION

Although the Reconstruction government lasted only seven years, the damage done by mismanagement guaranteed a hard time for the people of Henry County. The initial military government established the Freedman's Bureau that had noble intentions but was perverted by a number of circumstances. First and foremost, in its mission to educate and make productive citizens of the former slaves, it did not have the troop support it needed to insure the long-term protection of its charges. Many white Southerners of that generation simply did not like the enfranchisement of their former slaves and the poorest of the white farmers were especially alarmed because former slaves were now competing with them for the same jobs. As federal troops withdrew and Democrats started taking back control over local politics, they allowed and encouraged the suppression of the African-Americans and any whites who had been Union sympathizers during the war.

Above: A portrait of General William Sherman photographed by Matthew Brady.
COURTESY OF THE LIBRARY OF CONGRESS.

Below: Confederate palisades around Atlanta.
COURTESY OF THE LIBRARY OF CONGRESS.

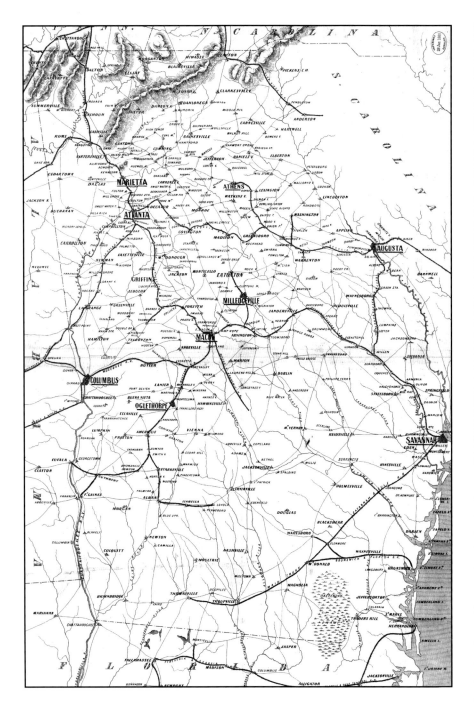

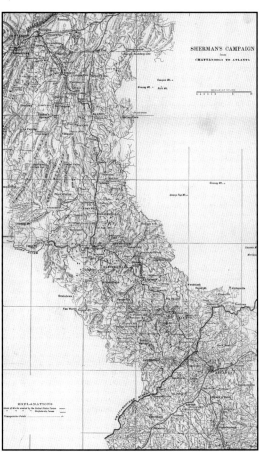

Above: An Army map of Georgia in 1864.

COURTESY OF THE LIBRARY OF CONGRESS.

Top, right: A map of Sherman's campaign through Georgia.

COURTESY OF THE LIBRARY OF CONGRESS.

Another problem during Reconstruction for Henry County was the economic situation. Many of the Henry County farmers were devastated by the war. They had lost all their agricultural stores and capital during the war. Both breeding and working livestock was also similarly devastated by the war. Many of the best families in Henry County had offered up their best and brightest sons to the Confederacy and many of these soldiers never came home. The Confederate money they had was useless. Overall, the average farmer had nothing to work with and not much, if any, money to purchase the needed seed, animals, or equipment to rebuild a farm. One of the major mistakes of the Reconstruction government was that it did not have any sort of long-term loan programs to help the people get back on their feet and the Georgia state constitution of 1870 prohibited the state from most major financial transactions that would have funded state rebuilding and investment projects. The farmers of Georgia were forced to mortgage many of their farms to banks, with the hope that they would be able to recoup the mortgage with one good cotton crop. But the fates would not be kind to these farmers. During the War, Europe had started buying its cotton cheaply from India and bought less from the United States. Also, the federal government imposed a per-bale tax that made Southern cotton more expensive than Indian cotton. The lack of revenue forced many farms into foreclosure and many former farmers were forced into being tenant farmers on land that had formerly been theirs. Some families decided to move west but the families that stayed would be, by the late 1870s, the beneficiaries of an era of prosperity that set the stage for modern Henry County.

CHAPTER IV

EARLY MODERN HENRY COUNTY, 1875-1941

After the agonizing years of war and rebuilding, the people of Henry County laid the foundation for Henry County as it is today. The people rebuilt Henry County with a new golden era of prosperity that lasted almost fifty years. But just as Henry County was standing tall as one of the most important counties in Georgia, it was hit with twin disasters that almost undid all the hard work of the previous half-century: the boll-weevil and The Great Depression.

BOURBONISM AND THE COTTON BOOM
THAT SAVED HENRY COUNTY

Henry County was in dire straits by the early 1870s. The hoped-for economic recovery after the Civil War never materialized. Many poor farmers had been forced to sell their farms and move to larger farms as either sharecroppers or tenant farmers. Compounding the economic problems were the freedmen whose numbers equaled or, at times, exceeded their former masters and were now competing for the same farm jobs. These dire economic circumstances forced some to emigrate to the newly opened lands in the West or, as many freedmen did, to emigrate to the economically healthier northern states. Luckily for the people of Henry County, a new brand of Democrats brought prosperity to Atlanta and directly helped the economic and social rejuvenation of Henry County.

The McDonough Train Depot.
COURTESY OF THE HENRY COUNTY
GENEAOLOGY SOCIETY.

As Republican Reconstruction governments lost power in 1871 and 1872, the state moved toward a virtual one-party rule by the Democrats. Almost as soon as the Democrats secured their power in the state, they started to factionalize. The first group made up of ex-Whigs and led by Robert Toombs and Alexander H. Stevens, was dedicated to restoring both the culture and society of antebellum Georgia. They were supported by newly forming agrarian associations, such as the Grange and the New Alliance, by preaching revocation of any Yankee influence in Georgia and warning of the 'plots' of freedmen and carpetbaggers who were actively keeping Georgia from returning to the agrarian utopia it had been before the Civil War.

The second group of Democrats, who initially called themselves the New Departure, but would later be better known as the Bourbons, believed in policy that they saw as an economically progressive platform that emphasized urban and industrial development. While the Bourbons were not actively against farming, they believed that the old day of cotton being king and Georgia as a predominantly agrarian economy were over and done with. Instead, they dreamed of building up the urban centers of Georgia by encouraging Northern investors to come to the south and build factories. The Bourbons believed that by building factories the people of Georgia could refine their raw natural resources, such as cotton and wood, into finished products. These finished products would sell for much more

than the raw resource and benefit the urbanite with more jobs and lower prices for finished goods, while also helping the rural farmer by raising the price of their raw resources. The Bourbons had their fair share of squabbles with other Democrats over this vision but they were strong enough to use these economic policies to rebuild Atlanta in record time and make it one of the economic powerhouses of the South.

The growth in Atlanta directly affected Henry County as the Bourbons actively developed the county as part of their economic experiment. In 1875, the financial center of Henry County was in the former town of Bear Creek, renamed Hampton in 1872, because of the rail station that passed through there. McDonough had barely more than three hundred souls in it and was only important for being the county seat. George Schaefer of Baltimore was sent down from Atlanta by cotton merchants. Schaefer established warehouses along the rail line in Hampton and Jonesboro. These warehouses were an economic godsend to the people of Henry County. As the Bourbons actively built up the textile factories in Atlanta and marketed Georgia cotton to Europeans, the price of cotton was going up. The people of Henry County were able to bring their cotton to market by using Schaefer's warehouses. Schaefer built additional warehouses in 1881 at Locust Grove and in McDonough the next year.

The next big economic boost for Henry County came when, on February 4, 1881, the State of Georgia decided to run an extension of the Atlanta-Macon rail line through McDonough.

By the time the rail line physically reached the town in June of the next year, McDonough was again, for the second time in its history a boomtown. One need only look at the economic development of McDonough to see how profound and quick this new prosperity was. In September 1881, McDonough was first reached by telegraph. In 1882, George Schaefer, in addition to his warehouse in McDonough, opened up a brick factory what would be the third opened up in that town in as many years.

By 1888, both of the newspapers in Henry County had relocated from Hampton to McDonough. In less than nine years McDonough had tripled its number of residents from a sleepy 325 in 1880 to nearly a thousand by 1889.

The cotton boom continued during the 1890s and 1900s and more businesses made their way to McDonough and benefited all of Henry County. Factories and machine shops opened in the town and provided employment and an escape for people who had been trapped in perpetual debt by tenant farming. By the early 1890s, another business mogul, Thomas D. Stewart, set up shop in Henry County and was influential in setting up the Bank of Henry County in 1896. A year earlier, McDonough put in its first streetlights and started work on its first water works facility. In 1887, work was started on the new county courthouse that still famously sits in McDonough's downtown square. As the price of cotton rose to eight cents a pound in 1889, more than double its lowest price during reconstruction, new innovations, such as the telephone and electric power, were assuring continued prosperity for the people of Henry County.

TWENTIETH CENTURY HENRY COUNTY

The prosperity of the last twenty-five years of the nineteenth century followed Henry County into the first two decades of the twentieth century. Economic prosperity continued unabated with Henry County's population growing to 20,420 in 1920, double the population a generation earlier in 1870. Public and private institutions flourished during this period.

Henry County had five schools that were giving first-class educations to the children of the county. The county's largest and most prestigious school, the Locust Grove Institute, was so well thought of in academic circles that many of its students were sent there from as far away as Europe. Graduates from the institute were regularly admitted to Ivy League colleges without the perfunctory entrance exams. While no longer a school, the Locust Grove Institute campus lives on today as the Locust Grove City Hall and features a museum dedicated to preserving the memories and artifacts of the institute.

Churches also boomed during this time. During the turn of the century, the three main religious denominations in Henry County expanded their congregations. Methodists, Baptists, and Presbyterians all made long-awaited improvements to older churches in the 1890s and started building additional churches to

Above: The Miller family blacksmith shop at White House, 1910.

Below: One of the historic homes in McDonough's Heritage Park.

satisfy the needs of new worshippers. The famous Shingleroof Campground, founded in 1830, was still one of the most important Methodist communal centers in Georgia, attracting many of the faithful during the late summer.

Henry County, because of her prosperity, was somewhat isolated from some of the economic pressures that sparked trouble in other parts of Georgia. The political and social revolutions pushed by the agrarian populist organizations of the 1890s made barely a ripple in Henry County. The economic prosperity kept both farm and factory worker working and satisfied.

The positive political effects of Henry County's economic prosperity could be seen as late as 1921 during the county's centennial celebrations. The second Ku Klux Klan, which had been recently resurrected in Athens and Atlanta and was all the rage in other Georgia counties, barely made a showing in Henry County. For the centennial celebrations the Klan could only muster a handful of people and, from an account of a contemporary commentator, one gets the impression that they were viewed as embarrassing eccentrics. This situation was quite different than some other Georgia counties that were virtually controlled by the Klan and would terrorize any person, of any ethnic background, who opposed their agenda.

About the only thing that did interrupt the rather idyllic existence in Henry County in the first two decades of the twentieth century was the First World War. The men of Henry County, being loyal citizens and truly brave, volunteered for the armed services without hesitation. Henry County signed up 1,607 men for service during the war years. The Army was quite happy to have the influx of soldiers from Georgia. They

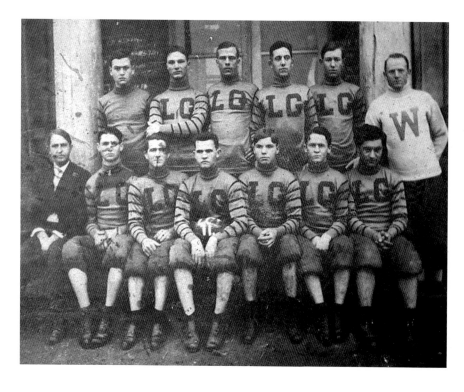

were in excellent physical shape from working on the farm and many of them made excellent sharpshooters thanks to experience hunting. Luckily, because of the brevity of American involvement in the First World War, many of the Henry County men who were inducted in the Army never made it out of Camp Gordon in Augusta, Georgia, and came back safety to their friends and family.

THE DECLINE OF HENRY COUNTY

The start of 1920 held high hopes for the people of Henry County. The economic prosperity and social progress of the county had continued in waves since 1875 and few thought the new decade would bring anything different. Unfortunately for the people of Henry County,

Above: Military cadets during World War I.
PHOTO BY CHRISTINE PARK HANKINSON. COURTESY OF THE HENRY COUNTY GENEAOLOGY SOCIETY.

Below: The Camp Creek train wreck on June 23, 1900.
COURTESY OF THE HENRY COUNTY GENEAOLOGY SOCIETY.

Top, left: Healthy cotton.

Top, right: A farm boy with a sack full of boll weevils which he has picked off of cotton plants.
PHOTO BY DOROTHEA LANGE. COURTESY OF THE LIBRARY OF CONGRESS.

Below: A cotton buyer's office, 1940.
PHOTO BY CHRISTINE PARK HANKINSON. COURTESY OF THE HENRY COUNTY GENEAOLOGY SOCIETY.

an alien invader would destroy almost every vestige of prosperity that had been built up in the past four-and-a-half decades. The invader to Henry County was the Cotton Boll Weevil. During the nineteenth century, the boll weevil had slowly made its way up from the jungles of southern Mexico to the border of Texas by 1892. Once the boll weevil reached South Texas it found an abundant food supply in cotton fields and was free to do as it wished since there were no natural predators of the boll weevil in the United States. Ten years after the boll weevil crossed the Rio Grande, its infestations had made it as far as the Louisiana border. Ten years after that, in 1912, the boll weevil reached the Georgia border. Some time in 1919, the first boll weevils entered Henry County. The next year they devastated the cotton harvest. The effects of the boll weevil invasion were immediate and devastating. When the 1920 harvest was destroyed, many farmers, whose yearly income was made during the harvest, were destitute. As the farmer's income dried up, all other sectors of business were devastated; and, in a pattern reminiscent of the Reconstruction, the banks started calling in their farm loans and for the second time in Henry County's history a large number of people lost their farms.

Cotton as an industry, both in Henry County and Georgia in general, started dying with the infestation of the boll weevil. In 1915, the entire state produced a record high of 2.8 million bales of cotton; by 1923 the state only produced six-hundred thousand bales. This decline continued until the 1980s, when the state produced only one-hundred and twelve thousand bales of cotton, the State of Georgia initiated an eradication program in 1987 that all but wiped out the boll weevil problem by 1990. By 1995, Georgia was again, for the first time in seventy

HENRY COUNTY AND THE GREAT DEPRESSION

years, in the forefront of cotton production with over two million bales of cotton produced.

Ironically, the initial reaction to the boll weevil from contemporary commentators has a tone of brash confidence. Even in 1921, the pervading wisdom seemed to be that the boll weevil crisis would blow over in some way, shape, or form. In this period the only method of fighting the boll weevil came in the form of arsenate poison in liquid or dust form. But the use of arsenic was not entirely effectively even when properly applied and there were many people who were quite reluctant to use the poison on their crops. With or without poison, the boll weevil was so voracious that it destroyed or significantly damaged every crop. The boll weevil managed to destroy not only the fortunes of farmers, it also closed the chapter on an era in Henry County's history. The farming of cotton, as an economic system and a way of life, was destroyed. Even though Henry County had other agricultural resources, such as its timber stocks and peaches, no other agrarian commodity, would ever produce the wealth that cotton did. All the high hopes of Henry County at the beginning of the 1920s had been dashed and one-fourth of the county's population left to find work in other parts.

Henry County, already reeling from the effects of the boll weevil invasion, took the events of the Great Depression in stride. The Great Depression had the same devastating effects that it had on the rest of the country. As with the previous decade, more jobs and businesses were lost in the county but unlike the economic downturn during the 1920s, few people left Henry County. The economic situation was so hopeless in the rest of the country that there was little point in moving away from Henry County. There were a number of public improvement projects, both federal and state, that helped develop the county's infrastructure and create jobs in the county. In 1931, State Highway 42 was paved and connected

Top, left: The abandoned Miller's Mill.
PHOTO BY RON & ALICE LEWIS. COURTESY OF THE HENRY COUNTY GENEAOLOGY SOCIETY.

Above: Equipment in the abandoned Miller's Mill.
PHOTO BY RON & ALICE LEWIS. COURTESY OF THE HENRY COUNTY GENEAOLOGY SOCIETY.

Below: Black sharecroppers working in a cotton field.
COURTESY OF THE LIBRARY OF CONGRESS

❖

Above: The bridge at Miller's Mill.
PHOTO BY RON & ALICE LEWIS. COURTESY OF
THE HENRY COUNTY GENEAOLOGY SOCIETY.

Top, right: The dam at Miller's Mill.
PHOTO BY RON & ALICE LEWIS. COURTESY OF
THE HENRY COUNTY GENEAOLOGY SOCIETY.

*Right: The Locust Grove Institute
building. The institute is now closed
and the Locust Grove City Hall is now
located in the building.*

McDonough to Atlanta. In 1938, federal funds allowed the building of the McDonough High School and a new library. The farmers who still had land tried to make a rebound by turning their cotton fields into peach orchards, cattle pastures and vegetable farms and this did bring some income into the county. These positive developments aside, Henry County had entered a state of economic suspended animation that would last until the 1950s. Not all was despair though; many of the elder residents of Henry County now remember with some fondness the memories of their families pulling together. In both social and church functions, the people of Henry County supported each other and had a real sense of community in a way that is rare in the contemporary hustle and bustle of modern-day life.

CHAPTER V

THE SECOND REVIVAL OF HENRY COUNTY, 1941 TO THE PRESENT

The 1920s and 1930s were some of the hardest years ever to visit the people of Henry County, but circumstances would start to get better for the people of Henry County. Henry County's recovery started slowly during the Second World War and would gain real strength in the following two decades. The slow economic regeneration of the county accelerated substantially in the 1970s with Interstate Highway 75 being built through the center of the county. In the 1980s, the growth of Atlanta as one of the major business centers of the world directly bought new businesses to Henry County. This period also saw major new residential growth as the phenomenon of suburban and satellite communities reached the county. All the positive economic factors and planning by state and local agencies came to full fruition in the 1990s when Henry County became the fourth-fastest growing county in the United States with an economic boom the scale of which has rarely been seen in the United States history.

An aerial view of McDonough, 1960.

THE LIGHT AT THE END OF THE TUNNEL: 1941-1954

The Henry County that was left by the men going off to the Armed Services after Pearl Harbor was a very quiet rural county. The 1940 Census reported only 15,119 souls, the large majority farmers

and agricultural markets to produce as much as they could at prices that were significantly better than the Great Depression years. The effect of this massive federal spending can be seen in Henry County with the decision made by Southern States, Inc. to open a textile and industrial electrical parts plant in the county. They were so impressed with the county, they decided to move their headquarters there after the war. Immediately after the war, in 1946, Robertson Furniture factory moved to Locust Grove; the McDonough Power Equipment, better known today as Snapper Mover, opened up in 1947; and the McDonough Foundry and Machine Company was also opened that same year. Companies such as these brought both badly needed jobs and income to the county.

One more factor in Henry County's recovery during and after the Second World War were the soldiers themselves. The veterans coming back from war had seen the outside world, learned technical skill in the armed services, and, perhaps most importantly, the United States passed the G.I. Bill that paid the college tuition of returning veterans. The effect the G.I. Bill had on both America and Henry County was amazing. The G.I. Bill allowed millions of people who would not have been able to afford college to become the first person ever in their families to receive a college degree. Once these veterans graduated, they came back to their old

and their families that had held on during the lean years of the past twenty years. The effects of the war and the men who served would have a profound effect on Henry County for the better.

The Second World War was the economic event that helped shake off the last vestiges of the Great Depression from the American landscape. The amount of raw supplies needed for the Allied War effort was enormous and the Federal Government started stockpiling these goods in 1939, two years before America joined the war. The effect of these industrial orders was to rejuvenate the sluggish manufacturing

communities wanting to make the most of their lives. This newly educated and energetic class provided the economy with the skills and attitude need to grow the county's economy into a new historic phase of growth.

NEW HOPE AND THE HIGHWAY: 1955-1979

The next great phase in Henry County's growth came about from three factors. The first factor was Atlanta's growth and the economic spillover to Henry County. Atlanta was becoming a hub for industry because of its business-friendly government and state tax policies that encouraged companies in other states to relocate to Georgia. So many people and companies had moved to Atlanta by the 1960s that it in many ways became its own self-sustaining economy that grew homegrown business designed to service the growing needs of companies, government institutions, and the general population. Henry County was the beneficiary of both public and private institutions wanting to do business in the Atlanta area without being physically located in Atlanta. In 1960 the FAA opened one of its major Air Traffic Control Centers in Hampton and has continued to expand this facility ever since. That same year, investors finished the famous Atlanta Motor Raceway.

The second factor affecting Henry County growth was the construction of Interstate Highway 75 through Henry County. I-75, which was part of the ambitious Interstate Highway Program that started in the 1950s under the Eisenhower administration, was planned to pass to the west of McDonough, Stockbridge, and Locust Grove. When this initial plan was announced in 1962, it initially generated a great deal of excitement, mainly positive, over the prospect of an Interstate Highway going through Henry County. By the time it was opened on October 15, 1969 it had already brought a number of roadside restaurants and hotels. As I-75 was one of the main arteries to and from Atlanta, more people would stop in Henry County to visit, shop, eat, or rest; and these traveler's dollars made a direct impact into the Henry County economy.

The final growth factor of this era was creation of the first professional economic-

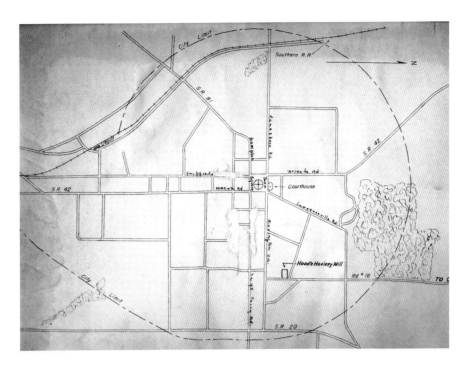

planning agency that was focused on sustaining the long-term growth of Henry County. In 1960 the Henry County Planning Commission was created with a view toward trying to channel Henry County's growth into productive areas and to act as liaisons between the community and prospective businesses that might be interested in moving to the county. Examples of their efforts in this period include: the discouragement of Atlanta's slums and junkyards from moving into northern Henry County; spearheading the County Water System that was

Above: A map of McDonough from the 1950s.
COURTESY OF THE HENRY COUNTY GENEALOGICAL SOCIETY.

Below: Atlanta Motor Speedway, 1970.
COURTESY OF THE HENRY COUNTY GENEALOGICAL SOCIETY.

built in the early 1970s; and the creation of industrial park areas so heavy industrial companies would have less of an impact on the communities in which they resided. The Henry County Planning Commission, along with the construction of I-75, and the growth of Atlanta all created a positive business climate that would

reach full bloom in the last two decades of the twentieth century.

HENRY COUNTY TRIUMPHANT: 1980 TO PRESENT

The growth of Atlanta and the friendly business climate of Henry County created a twenty-plus year period of growth that surpasses in scope and scale all the booms of the past. In the beginning of this period, in 1980, Henry County was still a largely rural county

Above: An aerial view of McDonough from 1971.
COURTESY OF THE HENRY COUNTY GENEALOGICAL SOCIETY.

Bottom, left: The Henry County Courthouse around 1970.
COURTESY OF THE HENRY COUNTY GENEALOGICAL SOCIETY.

Below: Eagles Landing Resort in McDonough.
COURTESY OF THE GEORGIA DEPARTMENT OF INDUSTRY, TRADE & TOURISM.

Above: Locust Grove police officers around 1970.
COURTESY OF THE HENRY COUNTY GENEALOGICAL SOCIETY.

Top, right: Newt Gingrich and the mayor of McDonough.
COURTESY OF THE HENRY COUNTY GENEALOGICAL SOCIETY.

Below: Hampton in the 1970s.
COURTESY OF THE HENRY COUNTY GENEALOGICAL SOCIETY.

with only thirty-six thousand souls in it. Twenty years later, in 2000, the county had 104,000 residents and, by 2003, there was an estimated population of 140,000. The growth of Henry County's population was directly related to Atlanta's emergence as an international city. In the 1980s, Atlanta, because of its friendly business climate, was becoming one of the preferred cities for companies that were looking to relocate. In addition to attracting Fortune 500 companies to the area, the friendly business climate allowed for local entrepreneurs to start up their own businesses and add to the collective wealth of the greater Atlanta economy. But, as Atlanta grew, many people who worked in the city yearned for the simpler life available in the country. This desire to live in small-town

America while working in the big city created the phenomenon of suburban bedroom communities. With I-75 running through the heart of the county, the towns of Henry County looked like the perfect place to put down roots. These new residents attracted new businesses, like Nestle, Ford, Nippon Electronics Company (NEC), Toys 'R Us, and, for a time, Amazon.com to the Henry County area. Local companies, most notably Snapper Mowers, were able to expand their customer base to a national level and create a steady foundation of manufacturing jobs in Henry County.

The difference with this latest economic boom in Henry County, compared to the county's other booms is that this one is economically diversified and its effects are permanent. Unlike the previous booms, which were tied to one exclusive economic factors of

❖

Top: A farmer from the 1970s.
COURTESY OF THE HENRY COUNTY GENEALOGICAL SOCIETY.

Above: Modern cotton production.
COURTESY OF THE GEORGIA DEPARTMENT OF INDUSTRY, TRADE & TOURISM.

Right: Snapper Lawnmowers, a Henry County original.
COURTESY OF THE HENRY COUNTY GENEALOGICAL SOCIETY.

land and cotton, this boom is spread across all industries and is a sign that Henry County has become part of the self-sustaining economy of Atlanta. This unprecedented prosperity has not come without its own share of difficulties, but the people of Henry County are working to overcome those obstacles. The difficulties surround the issue of preserving Henry County's past while accounting for the influx of new people and developments within the county. Many of the old-timers, while welcoming Henry County's new residents, do not want the charm of old Henry County to be lost in all the excitement of the economic growth. The Henry County Chamber of Commerce, the Henry County Planning Commission, and the municipal governments have been working with the local historic associations to help preserve the past. Heritage Park in McDonough and the Locust Grove Institute Museum are just two examples of how the people of Henry County have united to preserve the past while embracing the future. Working together, the people of Henry County are making the first years of the new millennia into a golden era to live and work in.

SHARING THE HERITAGE

historic profiles of businesses,

organizations, and families that have

contributed to the development and

economic base of Henry County

SPECIAL THANKS TO

The Den-Ric Corporation

PSM Enterprises

Sterling Motors

Walker Concrete

World Champion Fitness

CITY OF STOCKBRIDGE

Above: Old Railroad Station on Berry Street in late 1960s or early 1970s.

Below: The Stockbridge City Hall, 1993.

A traveling "Yankee schoolteacher" from Maine and one of the county's first churches are the roots from which the dynamic City of Stockbridge emerged.

Henry County was founded May 1, 1821. The Old Stockbridge Concord Methodist Church was organized in 1829 in the northern part of the county, and a settlement soon grew up around the church. The original Old Stockbridge was little more than a crossroads when it applied for a post office sometime before the beginning of the Civil War. Needing a name for the application, the citizens apparently decided to name their village and post office for a Professor Stockbridge. The first post office, granted April 5, 1847, was located on Old Stagecoach Road. The original postmaster's annual compensation was $2.42.

Levi Stockbridge was born in Maine in the early 1800's, owned property in Florida, and traveled often down the eastern seaboard between the two states. He taught school along the way, primarily in farming communities. Rumored to be the first schoolteacher in the area, he was widely recognized as a pioneer in the education profession. A very bright

gentleman with diverse interests, he also has been credited with inventing a particular type of fertilizer that was widely used during his lifetime. Letters and interviews with John Stockbridge, Levi's great-grandson, point strongly to the conclusion that Levi Stockbridge was the Professor Stockbridge for which the city was named.

One of the critical events that shaped the development of Stockbridge was the completion of the Southern Railroad. The year was 1881, the railroad was built to connect Macon and Atlanta, and because of the railroad, settlers who owned land in and around Old Stockbridge dramatically increased the price of their land. In fact, the prices were so inflated that the railroad would not purchase a tract for a depot. Two prominent Atlantans, John W. Grant and George W. Adair, came down and bought a tract about a mile south of Old Stockbridge and offered individual lots at a reasonable price. The railroad, along with many others, took quick advantage of this opportunity and purchased the lot that eventually held the depot and was to become the center of the present City of Stockbridge.

The Southern Railroad dismantled the original railroad depot in the late 1970's or early 1980's. It was located about 600 feet north of Highway 42 and US 23 as you cross the bridge.

Stockbridge was incorporated as a town in 1895 and as a city on August 6, 1920. Since incorporation as a city, Stockbridge has grown dramatically; but during the past two decades, the growth has skyrocketed. Two thousand people called the city home in 1980. In 2000 the population was approached ten thousand. Projections have the number of citizens doubling again in the next three to five years to more than twenty thousand. Forming the southeastern point of a triangle with the City of Atlanta and the world's busiest airport,

Above: An early 1900s barber shop. Notice the gaslights and the tobacco spittoons on the floor.

Below: Old City Hall, 1932.

Hartsfield Atlanta International, Stockbridge is strategically positioned for a very dynamic, but challenging, future.

Since the early 1970s, Mayor R. G. "Rudy" Kelley has expertly guided the city through this period of enormous growth with great skill and vision. Priding itself on a constant, enduring emphasis and dedication to elevating the quality of life of its citizens, the city is a progressive community with aggressive leadership.

Yet improving the quality of life for citizens of a rapidly expanding suburban city, in close proximity to the tremendous growth engines of Atlanta and its huge airport, is no easy task. A beautiful and functional system of city parks, a planned town center providing the amenities and ease of access consistent with cutting-edge philosophy in community planning, and dramatic, recently completed city and convention centers—are proof of Mayor Kelley's and the city leadership's success to this point, and their future commitment to this daunting challenge.

Clark Park, named for Jim Clark, Gardner Park, named for W. A. "Rip" Gardner, Memorial Park, dedicated to Reverend Ferdinand Hunter, Joe Simmons and John Dabney—each offer

beautiful, relaxing respites from the hectic pace of everyday life, as well as numerous recreational activities. Walking trails, playgrounds, pavilions, basketball and tennis courts are available. Dabney, Hunter, and Simmons Memorial Parks are dedicated to deceased city council members.

Clark Park is adjacent to the magnificent Stockbridge Community and Conference Center, reminiscent of an elegant hunting lodge, which had a grand opening in March of 2002. The Merle Manders Conference Center has over 16,000 square feet of meeting rooms and classrooms, complete with outlets for computers, a beautiful, 6,500 square foot main ballroom with fireplace, stunning views of the park, and a state-of-the-art catering kitchen. The Conference Center was booked for months in advance with weddings, meetings and various events, even before its official opening. Following a precedent set in 1993 with the opening of a new City Hall, the Stockbridge Conference Center was paid for, in full, in cash, when it opened; another testament to dynamic and efficient leadership and vision of Mayor Kelley and the City Council.

The future of Stockbridge holds great promise, according to City Manager Ted Strickland. The planned city center, which will be the essence of a highly functional, pedestrian-oriented, retail and commercial center, will be only one of the most visible of numerous changes planned for the city over the next decade. New residential developments to compliment the highly acclaimed Eagles Landing, smart-growth remedies for traffic and density issues, the continuing annexation and expansion of the City–are but a few of these changes. Strickland is adamant that through the growth, development and change, the mission of the City's leadership will remain: a steadfast commitment to provide its citizens the best in planning and implementation, information and education, responsible economic development, history and heritage preservation, beautification, reforestation, and environmental protection, and expeditious responses to the changing needs of the community.

Above: A home on North Henry Boulevard that was built in the late 1800s or early 1900s.

Below: The Merle Mander Conference Center on Davis Road, 2002.

SNAPPER, INC.

It's always been about blades. Whether it was honing blades to cut down Georgia pines or developing revolutionary lawn mower blades—Snapper's roots cut deep into the Georgia soil.

The Snapper story began before the turn of the last century when most lawn mowers were livestock. Frank Ohien and Clarence Chaffe founded what is now Snapper, Inc. in 1890. Incorporated as Southern Saw Works on November 1, 1894 the company made circular saws for the growing Georgia lumber industry. For almost sixty years, as lumber prospered so did Southern Saw.

But by 1949, saw making was an industry in decline. William R. Smith, now the owner of Southern Saw, watched as green lawns replaced towering pines and made an insightful decision to enter the lawn mower industry. He purchased the patents of "Snappin' Turtle" mowers, one of the first rotary mowers, then built in Florida. Georgia production began in East Point in January 1951, when 16 of the unique mowers were shipped. By the end of 1951, a total of 3,975 mowers were manufactured and delivered throughout the United States. Several of these first mowers are on display at the Smithsonian Institute in Washington, D.C., and the Atlanta History Museum.

In the early 1950s, lawn mowers were a "growing" business. During the 1950s and 1960s, as lawn sizes grew from the postage lots in the city to the half-acre or more lots of the suburbs, homeowners were spending more of their recreation time mowing grass. Power reel mowers were expensive, heavy and awkward to handle. Their open reel made safety a continuing concern.

On January 16, 1951, Snapper introduced its "Snappin' Turtle," the first self-propelled rotary mower. Its smaller, lighter engine and safe, covered blade revolutionized the industry. A lower, more compact body made with new, less expensive yet stronger materials brought the price to a reasonable level.

As the mower business grew, the saw business waned. Soon, lawn mower manufacturing replaced saw production in the plant. In 1954 the decision was made to merge Southern Saw Works and the McDonough Foundry & Machine Works and move the entire operation to McDonough in Henry County. The merger of the two manufacturers created a new company known as McDonough Power Equipment.

Snapper mowers were leading a new revolution in lawn care equipment, and McDonough Power was growing with this revolution. Innovations in power mowers and accessories, many designed by Snapper, fueled the growth of rotary mowers and McDonough Power's line of consumer products. In fact, Snapper owns 44 patents for innovations in safety, deck design and transmissions.

❖

Above: William R. Smith.

Below and opposite: Advertisements for Snapper, Inc. products.

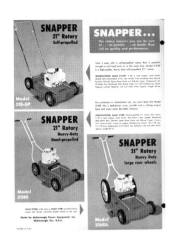

As lawns got bigger and leisure time got shorter, even self-propelled walk-behind mowers couldn't cut grass fast enough. So Snapper engineers designed and produced the Snapper rear-engine-riding mower. It gave consumers a machine priced between a walk-behind mower and its more expensive cousin, the lawn tractor. In its early production the Comet—named in the midst of the space race—replaced the traditional steering wheel with handlebars similar to those on a bicycle. At one time, Comet sales were more than eighty percent of McDonough Power transactions.

The success of the Comet and other products made Snapper an attractive acquisition, and in 1967, Snapper was purchased by Atlanta-based Fuqua Industries. The alliance provided Snapper with the capital to expand to a second manufacturing plant in Texas and continue the development of new and innovative additions to its product line, including lawn tractors in 1982 and rear-tine tillers and snow throwers in 1983. Building on its growing product/name recognition, McDonough Power was renamed Snapper Power Equipment in 1982.

Between 1982 and 1987, Snapper was growing almost twice as fast as the industry. During 1985 the McDonough plant was building a mower every fifty-two seconds

to keep up with demand. Commercial equipment was added to the Snapper mix in 1987 and the company used its creativity in the residential market to redefine the standards for commercial mowers.

As the decade progressed, Snapper developed inventive products such as the hydrostatic rear-engine rider and tractor and the Ninja® mulching system to answer consumer demands for better and more earth-friendly mowing systems.

In 1997 Snapper introduced its biggest innovation yet—Yard Cruiser®. A variation on the rear-engine rider, the Yard Cruiser® is a zero-turn radius mower providing the ultimate in comfort with single-hand, joystick steering. Snapper's latest product is the Grounds Cruiser Utility Vehicle introduced in 1999.

After more than 50 years, the company has grown to be a leader in the industry, with approximately 900 employees housed in nearly one million square feet of facilities in McDonough, Georgia. Major distribution centers outside of Georgia are located in Texas, Nevada, and Ohio. Snapper products are sold nationwide and abroad through over forty-eight hundred servicing dealers and Wal-Mart stores.

What started with a commitment to innovation and quality has persevered through the years.

BELLAMY-STRICKLAND AUTO DEALERS

The Bellamy-Strickland legacy began in 1982 as Bellamy Chevrolet under the dynamic leadership of Otis and Clifford Bellamy. Previously owned and operated as Bellamy Walker Chevrolet, the famous dealership has been known as Bellamy-Strickland Chevrolet since June of 1991. The company has acquired a host of important additions since its foundation—franchises such as Oldsmobile and GMC joined the family in 1994, while Pontiac joined the company in 1997. The Bellamy-Strickland Collision Center was purchased in January of 1999.

Throughout the past decade, outstanding growth and consistent expansion has been the motivating factor at Bellamy-Strickland. The number of employees has grown from 31 to 160. The new Pontiac-GMC building opened in January 2001 and specializes in Quick Lube and Quick Service items and boasts a state-of-the-art car wash.

Investing time and financial support into the community, Bellamy-Strickland remains involved with the Henry County Chamber of Commerce and contributes finances to a number of charities, including A Friend's House, Noah's Ark, the American Cancer Society, Habitat for Humanity, Henry County Council on Aging, Greater Henry County Education Foundation, Speedway Children's Charities, Flint River Council Boy Scouts of America, Shrine Circus Fund and local schools and churches.

The mission of Bellamy-Strickland is to be the most respected dealership among both customers and employees and to maintain a personal atmosphere between a diversified base

of commercial and retail customers that rely on them to satisfy their transportation needs. They desire to develop a reputation as an excellent place to work with a spirit among all employees that "these are our customers and our future depends on their complete satisfaction."

Bellamy-Strickland is located just minutes minutes south of Hartsfield International Airport off I-75 at Highway 155 in McDonough. At www.bellamystrickland.com, you will be introduced to their fine sales staff and have the opportunity to view new and used cars.

In 2001, William Strickland purchased the company from the Bellamy brothers. Loyal customers and outstanding employees have continued to make Bellamy-Strickland the leader among area dealerships in growth, sales and customer service. The dealership continues to pride themselves in providing excellent customer service that remains consistent long after the initial purchase.

HENRY COUNTY PUBLIC SCHOOLS

Designated as the sixth fastest-growing county in the United States, unprecedented growth continues to be a motivating factor in the life of Henry County Schools. After a one-cent sales tax increase in September 1997 and bond referendum in March 2000 for school construction, the school system was able to launch a building program that resulted in the opening of two new elementary schools in 1999 and another elementary, two middle schools, and one high school in 2000. Property has been acquired for an additional middle school and high school projected to open in 2002 and 2003.

This remarkable growth seems appropriate for a school system that traces its educational roots back to 1850. In her extensive account of the evolution of Henry County, *The Mother of Counties*, Vessie Thrasher Rainer found that in the early 1900s there were three schools in McDonough—the McDonough Institute, also known as the Miss Tippi School, and McDonough High School, also known as Ham School, and a large, two-story school building erected by the black population of McDonough.

When the McDonough Institute building was sold to the town's board of education in December of 1904, the new McDonough Public School would soon become a reality. McDonough High School was also closed as the City of

McDonough School opened its doors one month later on January 9, 1905 to 160 students and a monthly entrance fee of fifty cents for primary grade children, seventy-five cents for grammar students, and one dollar for high school students. The McDonough Consolidated High School building was opened in the 1938-1939 school year and included 11 full grades and a teaching faculty of 20.

After the opening of McDonough Primary School in the 1950s, the facility was renamed Henry County High School. Stockbridge High School opened its doors to

eager students in 1964 and a new Henry County Senior High School was created in 1972, along with a number of lower grade schools opening in other areas of the county.

Today, record numbers of new students are enrolling in the Henry County School System. The number of students attending Henry County Schools has risen to over twenty-nine thousand and reflects the stellar growth that has taken place in the population of Henry County. At this rate of growth, the school system population is projected to exceed forty thousand by 2006. With enrollment projections in mind, the Board of Education plans to build an additional 12 new schools over the next 6 years and several existing schools have been renovated and/or expanded to add more classroom space.

With about twenty-seven hundred outstanding employees, the Henry County Public School System could well be considered the largest business in Henry County. And this is important business—providing children with the skills and knowledge as they enter the world of the twenty-first century.

The commitment to recruiting and training top quality professional and support staff can be seen in the week-long orientation process that has won state and national acclaim. There is also a strong commitment to continuously review and strengthen every school's academic program by placing special emphasis on improving the use of instructional technology, improving student attendance, and challenging students to meet higher expectations, both in the world of academics and within the community.

The Department of Technology Services supports the provision of quality technology support and services for the purposes of improving student achievement of the Quality Core Curriculum through the use of technology. Our vision is for students to be prepared to succeed in the twenty-first century using telecommunications and technology resources to enhance personal achievement.

CITY OF LOCUST GROVE

These photos show the Academic Building of Locust Grove Institute in 1923, complete with steeple (below), and in 1988 (right). The old steeple was made of wood, the new one of aluminum. The new steeple cost approximately $25,000.

Tradition and change are as common in the City of Locust Grove as the impressive groves of locust trees that adorn this tranquil community. Historically, the town's first store was built on Main Street in 1870. Three cotton gins and several warehouses sustained the community, as it would become a major rail distribution center for cotton, peaches, and other farm products.

Officially incorporated on December 20, 1893, the original city limits extended a quarter-mile in every direction from the train depot in the heart of town and its government consisted of one mayor and five council members—they included Mayor M. P. Sowell and council members G. P. Combs,

C. M. Mahone, J. L. Gardner, R. C. Brown, and W. H. Peek. C. W. Williams served as the first city clerk. The first ordinance passed by the city council restricted the speed of the trains to fifteen miles per hour. There were questions on how to enforce this because the city did not have a police department at that time, but the railroad was notified.

One of Henry County's most important landmark buildings is the Locust Grove Institute (LGI), founded by The Locust Grove Baptist Church and Mercer University. In 1894 the first building of the Institute was erected and the school opened its doors on November 1, 1894 with thirteen students and two instructors. The end of the school year had enrolled eighty-five students. LGI grew rapidly and several houses in the community, such as the Combs-McKnight-Morfoot House were used as boarding houses to help accommodate the growing student population.

Locust Grove Institute served a very important purpose by providing top-notch college preparatory classes and was one of the first schools in Georgia to be accredited by the Association of Schools and Colleges of the Southern States. The curriculum stressed learning in all facets of life, but its primary goal was character building. The academic building was constructed in 1904 for a total cost of $14,000. The original building was destroyed by fire in

1906. LGI began a military training program for its students in 1918 and, in 1919; the Institute transferred all property titles to the Georgia Baptist Convention. During this period of time, Locust Grove was reincorporated as a new charter was established for the city in 1922.

The Great Depression and the introduction of public schools in Henry County led to the demise of The Locust Grove Institute in May of 1930. The school remained empty until 1936 when the academic building served as a public elementary school for the city. In 1983 the City of Locust Grove purchased the building. Numerous renovations were made and the structure was restored, modifying the interior to house the various City Government offices, presently known as the Locust Grove Municipal Complex. This building was entered on the National Register of Historic Places on September 4, 1986.

Locust Grove has recently experienced a growth in population and in the businesses coming into the area. In 1900 the population of the city was 254. According to the latest census figures the city population has grown to 2,322. After the Tanger Outlet Mall opened in 1994, many new businesses have made Locust Grove their home. Our city has a strong heritage and our roots are firmly planted. Our blossoming community looks forward to the future with great expectations.

Working together with its residents, the City of Locust Grove strives to provide an open, accessible, responsive, and fiscally responsible government to ensure the city remains a premier place in which to live, work and spend leisure time.

Residents recognize the city's continued dedication to all areas affecting the quality of life as they strive to ensure balanced and responsible urban design, planning and development, and protection of the city's historical, cultural, and natural resources.

The city's efforts are targeted to ensure a vibrant economic climate that will attract and support a diversity of business opportunities and community services. The city continues in a commitment to excellence in maintaining its "TREASURES"—a small, friendly and safe town; a good environment in which to raise a family; the preservation of traditions and natural resources; recreation and cultural opportunities; and employment opportunities.

Most importantly, the City of Locust Grove remains dedicated to serving each and every resident as they endeavor to create a beautiful town in which anyone would be proud to call home.

❖

Above: Public works employees David (Jap) Colbert and Kenny McIntyre standing beside the city's new chipper truck.

Below: Captain Swanson and Chief Patton standing next to the city's police cruiser, ready to protect and serve their community.

SMITH, WELCH & BRITTAIN

❖

Top, left: E. M. Smith.

Top, right: Ernest M. Smith.

Below: An artist's rendering of the original offices on Keys Ferry Street in McDonough, Georgia.

Smith, Welch & Brittain is among Henry County's oldest law firms, having held and maintained the highest professional competency rating recognized in the legal profession. For over a century the firm has been dedicated to client satisfaction by providing quality legal services in an ethical and cost efficient manner.

The firm traces its origins back to 1890, when E. M. Smith began his law practice in McDonough, Georgia, having graduated from law school at the University of Georgia. His son, Ernest M. Smith, followed in his father's footsteps, and in 1970 formed the partnership that continues to this day. Ernest served his community in a number of capacities prior to devoting himself to the practice of law.

For example, while Ernest graduated with honors from the University of Georgia with an AB degree in 1931 and a law degree in 1934, upon his return to McDonough, he served as its mayor from 1935 to 1940, as a member of the House of Representatives from 1937 to 1940, and as a member of the Senate in 1941 and 1942. He also served as the county attorney from 1937 to 1942 until he departed for Washington, D.C., where he was admitted to the District of Columbia Bar Association in 1949. He was appointed by President Harry S. Truman to the U.S. Motor Carrier Claims Commission and served there until 1952. Upon the completion of his duties for President Truman, he returned to McDonough and served as the Henry County attorney from 1955 to 1972.

In 1970, A. J. (Buddy) Welch returned home to McDonough after receiving his AB degree from the University of Georgia and his juris doctorate law

degree from Mercer University and joined the firm. Buddy and Ernest practiced together at Smith & Welch until Smith's death on April 10, 1992.

In the interim, two more lawyers, Ben W. Studdard, III, (who would later become the first State Court Judge of Henry County) and J. Mark Brittain became partners. While the '90s began inauspiciously with the devastating loss of its founding partner, that passing marked not the end, but the beginning of a new and exciting period in the firm's history. Subsequent to this time, the firm continued to experience significant growth bringing forth the admission of E. Gilmore

Maxwell, J. Byrd Garland, T. Bruce McFarland, and John P. Webb as partners.

Smith, Welch & Brittain has grown as Henry County has grown. In 1995 a second office, in Stockbridge, was opened with Mark Brittain assigned as managing partner at that location. In 2001 the Garland Law Firm of Jackson, Georgia (formerly Garland & Milam), merged with Smith, Welch & Brittain, thereby establishing a third office, with Byrd Garland named as its managing partner. In October 2003, another office for the Jackson operation opened at the corner of Georgia Highway 16 and Georgia Highway 42 leading into Jackson. A fourth and fifth office were also opened in 2003 in Barnesville and Peachtree City, respectively. Smith, Welch & Brittain, having started out as a two-man operation off the McDonough Square in the early 1930s, now employs 18 lawyers and 88 support personnel in 5 offices throughout Henry, Butts, Lamar, and Fayette Counties.

Smith, Welch & Brittain is a full service law firm. The attorneys practice in most areas of civil and criminal litigation, including personal injury, medical malpractice, worker's compensation, family law (including divorce and adoption), employment law, business law, local government law, condemnation/eminent domain proceedings, all aspects of commercial and residential real estate transactions, condominium, cooperative and homeowner association law, contractor/builder/homeowner disputes and DUI/criminal defense.

Above: A. J. (Buddy) Welch.

Below: An artist's rendering of the current offices of Smith, Welch & Brittain at 2200 Keys Ferry Court in McDonough, Georgia.

COUNTRY INN & SUITES

Located at 115 East Greenwood Road in McDonough, Country Inn & Suites represents one of the newest hotels in the area with 57 rooms and 24 suites. Construction began in January 2001 and the hotel opened its door to customers on September 1, 2001.

When you walk into the Country Inn & Suites, you will experience a sitting area flooded with warm sunlight, hardwood floors and fireplace; a great place for conversation or just sitting back and enjoying a good book! Built with the business and leisure traveler in mind, the hotel is a cut above the rest. Besides having a great location, the Country Inn & Suites–McDonough is truly one of the nicest hotels for business in this area.

While relaxing in the beautiful lobby, the hotel encourages its guests to enjoy some of its wonderful freshly baked cookies twenty-four hours a day. In each room, guests enjoy access to a microwave, refrigerator, coffee makers, hairdryer, full length ironing board and iron, data port, two-line phone, and cable television. The hotel also has an indoor pool, Jacuzzi, and exercise facility, and offers a complimentary deluxe breakfast.

Country Inn & Suites–McDonough is conveniently located 8 miles from the famed Atlanta Motor Speedway and approximately 25 miles from the historic Georgia Dome, Turner Stadium, the Atlanta Zoo, CNN Center, World Congress Center, and Centennial Olympic Park. Golfing, shopping, tennis, and a wide range of eateries will ensure that your stay at Country Inn & Suites is memorable.

You can obtain further information about the hotel at www.countryinn.com. Country Inn & Suites also has a central reservations number that is accessible anywhere in the United States and is available to anyone who wants to make reservations 24 hours a day, 7 days a week.

Country Inn & Suites values its guests and offers excellent service to attract its guests back to its hotel again and again. The goal at Country Inn & Suites–McDonough is to make you feel like you are at home when you are staying at the hotel. For reservations please call the hotel directly at 770-957-0082. Book your room today!

Country Inn & Suites…it's a lot like home.

❖

Above: A delicious continental breakfast awaits guests each and every morning at Country inn & Suites.

Below: An indoor swimming pool and Jacuzzi allows guests to relax and enjoy their stay in McDonough.

CANNON–CLEVELAND FUNERAL DIRECTORS

Top, left: The former Rainer-Carmichael Funeral Home in McDonough, Georgia.

Top, right: The former Rainer Funeral Home in Stockbridge, Georgia.

Below: The new location of Cannon Cleveland Funeral Directors.

Henry County's "hometown" funeral home is back home again. After a long and storied history, local businessmen Greg Cannon, Donald Cleveland, and Peter Thornton returned the county's renowned, premier funeral home to local ownership. "It was important to improve the level of service available to Henry County families, and establish more of a community oriented business," states Greg Cannon.

The roots of Cannon-Cleveland go back to 1940 and the establishment of the Carmichael Funeral Home by D. T. Carmichael. The original business was located in the Amasa Spencer House, built in 1835 in McDonough. D. T. Carmichael & Sons Funeral Home remained in business until 1977 when it was purchased by Fred and Ray Rainer and renamed the Rainer-Carmichael Funeral Home. They established a second location, the Rainer Funeral Home, in Stockbridge, in 1991. In the late 1990s, SCI, a Texas-based funeral home acquisition company, purchased both locations.

In 1999, employees Greg Cannon, Donald Cleveland, and Peter Thornton purchased both funeral homes back from SCI, changing the name to Cannon-Cleveland Funeral Directors. Plans were immediately launched for a new facility to replace the two existing locations.

In March 2000 a groundbreaking was held for the new facility at the intersection of Highway 42 North and Braman Road in McDonough. On October 15, 2000, an open house and dedication ceremony was held for the new funeral home. Local architect Roger Moss designed the 11,800 square-foot facility. It features a spacious chapel, four viewing rooms, a family lounge, children's room and approximately 130 parking spaces.

According to Cannon, Cleveland, and Thornton, their goal is exemplary service, at a fair price, in a time of need. "I look at it as really a ministry to people," states Cleveland. "They come in here hurt and devastated, and our responsibility is to listen and let them express their feelings. Our responsibility is to provide them with the services they want."

In keeping with the Cannon–Cleveland spirit of offering only the finest in dedicated, highly personal service for their clients, community service also plays a big role at this company. There is employee involvement in Rotary, Kiwanis, Knights of Columbus, various churches, and the company is a member of the Henry County Chamber of Commerce, McDonough Business Association and the Georgia Funeral Directors Association.

Henry County's "hometown" funeral home truly is back home again. Providing personal, professional service that began many years ago, now in a modern facility, with the credo—Remembering the Past...Serving the Future.

ALH Nursery in McDonough is bringing excitement to the business of enhancing the Georgia landscape. In business since 1995, gardening and landscape design are the specialty of Gary Mosley, Greg Davis, Adam Lobrano, and their team of knowledgeable and experienced personnel. Noted throughout Henry County for its consistently outstanding customer service and competitive pricing, the company stands at the forefront of the industry as they couple old-fashioned hometown service with modern design and the very latest in green industry certification.

Customers who find themselves interested in any aspect of landscape and design can be assured that the first relationship with ALH will be a lasting one. Certified personnel work closely with each customer from the outset—through the process of a free design consultation to the final creation of a landscape that meets the needs of each individual. Every investment is tailored to the specific needs of each client and questions are answered with accuracy and honesty.

The delight of every gardener in Henry County will be met while browsing through the wide range of ornamental trees, fruit trees, ornamental shrubs, perennials, annuals, bulbs, and hanging baskets that line the greenhouses of ALH Nursery. Grass seeds, fertilizers, mulches, pest control products, weed control products as well as a host of ideas and tools await the eager customer.

ALH NURSERY, INC.

❖

Top: Home of free design consultation.

Middle: Color is our speciality.

Bottom: ALH employees at the Oakland Elementary Fall Festival.

By visiting ALH Nursery, Inc. on the Internet you can learn more about the company and how they might enhance your landscaping needs as well as help you save money with special offers. Please visit www.alhnursery.com for further details.

McDonough First United Methodist Church

As the twenty-first century visitor enters the sanctuary doors of this historic Henry County church and is warmly greeted by a host of welcoming handshakes and friendly faces, the mission and ministry of McDonough First United Methodist Church is apparent. From the pristine steeple to the tolling bells that herald the community to join the congregation in worship in Sunday School and at one of two services held each Sunday morning, the church has weathered the changes of time and history for two centuries proclaiming the timeless Gospel message.

According to the historical record of J.P. Price, Henry County was in its infancy in 1822 when fellow worshippers from various denominations met on the southwest corner of the public square to hold religious services. A strong Methodist congregation began to grow in the county as

❖

Right: McDonough First United Methodist Church, c. 1905.

Below: McDonough First United Methodist Church, c. 1965.

McDonough was incorporated in 1823. Names such as Allen and Wade Turner and Tandy Key are synonymous with frontier Methodism and its increasing influence in the community.

A plot of land was purchased in 1830 and became the first site for a Methodist Church in McDonough, served by circuit-riding preachers along the Yellow River Mission.

A wooden frame church was built in 1894 and replaced by a modern brick facility completed in June 1905. As outstanding pastors and their families weaved their way through the history and lives of First Methodist Church, additions to the church continued with a new educational building in 1953 and completion of the present sanctuary in 1965. A new Sunday school building with a fellowship hall was dedicated in April 1982.

The church continued its steady growth as it began a capital stewardship campaign in 1997 that resulted in the creation of an entirely new mission church at its property along John Wesley Way. After families from the church agreed to become the core membership of the Wesley Way United Methodist Church, McDonough First United Methodist Church was honored at the North Georgia Annual Conference in 2001 with the "Mother Church of the Year" award.

For more information about services and times as well as photos and detailed information regarding the mission programs and exciting ministries of McDonough First United Methodist Church, please visit www.mcdonoughumc.org.

SOUTHERN STATES, LLC

Southern States, LLC represents almost a century of innovation in the design and manufacture of high voltage switching equipment ranging from 15,000 volts to 1.1 million volts. The company's broad scope of products for the electrical power industry includes air disconnect switches, power fuses, circuit switchers, and the recently patented LLS Load & Line Switchers. You will find Southern States' equipment at work in substations around the world, helping to deliver energy safely and efficiently.

Southern States employs about three hundred people from Henry County and surrounding areas. Its main facility consist of 160,000 square feet of manufacturing, operations,and office space, plus a high-voltage test lab. The company is an active member of the Henry County Chamber of Commerce and a supporter of numerous community and charitable activities.

Strong financial and human resources along with a state-of-the-art facility support the company's goal of helping customers find cost-effective, targeted solutions for all their switching needs. Meeting "needs" is readily seen in Southern States innovative product and service developments and in the one hundred-plus patents held by the company.

Southern States was founded in 1916, when W. E. Mitchell opened a repair shop to service electrical motors and transformers in Birmingham, Alabama. The young company continued to expand with motor operators being its first manufactured product.

As a contributing member of the war effort, Southern States purchased Henderson Foundry & Machine Works in Hampton, Georgia to manufacture munitions in 1940. The plant also continued to produce its existing line of textile machine parts. At the end of the war, Southern States consolidated its operations at the Georgia facility.

Today, Southern States operates in a highly electrical-dependent world—a world dealing with deregulation, rapid technological developments, and increasing global

competition. It is a world of change. In its well-established tradition of leadership, Southern States embraces the challenge of providing the innovation and advancements required to reach the future.

Type LLS Load & Line Switcher (above) rated 242 kV and Type EV-1 Vertical Break Disconnect Switch (below) rated 550 kV.

ECOLAB

A true visionary trying to create better soap products in the early 1920s gave birth to Ecolab, the leading global developer and marketer of premium cleaning, sanitizing, pest elimination, and service solutions for the hospitality, institutional and industrial markets. The McDonough plant opened in 1988.

Today, the local plant, including office and warehouse space totals 175,000 square feet and has 100 employees. With the help of a distribution plant in Orlando, Florida, the plant services the southeast region of the United States.

M. J. Osborn founded Economics Laboratory in St. Paul, Minnesota at the beginning of an age of remarkable expansion in the restaurant and lodging industries. He started out with only one product—a carpet cleaner called "Absorbit," his second product was "Soilax" developed for the new electric dishwashers. His determination to build on his dream, despite early struggles to find backers, paid off as the company grew and expanded its product line for restaurants, hotels and motels. Additional markets include hospitals, food and beverage plants, laundries, schools, and other industrial and institutional markets.

Ida C. Koran was the first employee, working with Osborn as secretary, office manager, and sometimes assistant in the factory, shipping daily sales of five barrels of soap. She ended her career as corporate secretary and member of the board of directors. The success of the company created a personal fortune that she bequeathed to help company associates who experienced hardship. Today the Ida C. Koran Foundation also provides scholarships for children of employees worldwide.

Ecolab's global headquarters remains in St. Paul, Minnesota. The company operates in 70 countries, employing 20,000 associates and reaches customers in more than 100 other countries through distributors, licensees, and export operations. Under the leadership of CEO Al Schuman, the company has more than doubled in size since 1995, to approximately $3 billion annually, making it one of the *Fortune 1000* largest companies. Today there are more than fifty state-of-the-art Ecolab manufacturing and distribution facilities worldwide.

The company's mission statement reflects its unwavering commitment to the highest standards of innovation and service:

"Our business is to be the leading innovator, developer and marketer of worldwide services, products and systems, which provide superior value to our customers in meeting their cleaning, sanitizing and maintenance needs, while conserving resources, preserving the quality of the environment and providing a fair profit for our shareholders."

In addition to substantial employment and economic benefits to the community, the McDonough Ecolab plant provides funding for various nonprofit organizations including food banks, scholarship programs, pediatric care for children, AIDS, literacy, and elderly care. Funding for schools' K-12 programs and employees' active participation in the local United Way are also a part of the company's dedication to community and charitable services.

Hampton Inn of McDonough was founded in 1995, joining the historically rich, illustrious family of Hilton hotels. With more than twelve hundred locations, Hampton Inns are the nation's leading chain of quality, value priced hotels. J.D. Powers and Associates have rated Hampton Inns number one in guest satisfaction for four straight years.

Located on Interstate 75 at mile marker 218, approximately thirty miles south of the mega-metropolis of Atlanta, the Hampton Inn is a quick six miles from Tanger Factory Outlet and its sixty-five outlet stores, eight miles from the NASCAR mania of Atlanta Motor Speedway, and just over twenty miles from Atlanta Hartsfield International, the world's largest airport.

According to General Manager Sid Roach, the hotel is renowned for both the "best hotel breakfast in McDonough," and its role for the past four years as host to the competitors of a major LPGA tour event. The Chick Filet Championship is played in April at the Eagle Landing Country Club, a short drive from the Hampton.

The hotel has 74 rooms, a conference room, a pool, and exercise facilities; and provides fax and photo copying service, 75 cable channels, including HBO, and children under 18 stay free when accompanied by their parents. Complimentary breakfasts, copies of USA Today, free local calls to three million people, and tea and coffee in the lobby are other popular features of the Hampton Inn McDonough. There are also rooms available for wheelchair-dependent guests.

"We are firmly committed to friendly, efficient service and attention to our guests needs in a first-rate lodging environment," states Roach. "Living up to the lofty standards of Hilton and Hampton is a given here. Our goal is to exceed those standards."

Hampton Inn is located at 855 Industrial Parkway in McDonough, Georgia.

STRINGER LUMBER COMPANY

❖

Above: Aerial view of Stringer Lumber Company.

PHOTOGRAPH COURTESY OF AERIAL VIEWS, INC.

Below: Stringer Lumber Company is located at 18 Lyman Stringer Boulevard in McDonough, Georgia.

Stringer Lumber Company has developed into one of the leading suppliers of home building materials in Henry County. It wasn't always that way.

"Don't set that lumber down for long, it'll sink right down into the mud." According to founder Lyman Stringer, that was the joke when he opened his lumberyard on 1.25 acres of unpaved land in the City of McDonough, Henry County, Georgia, in 1972. Along with partner Bert Johnson and the sales staff of Gerald Stone and Howard Jones, Stringer and the fledgling company strived to build a loyal, and profitable, customer base. "Most of the business in the early years was in Atlanta and Fulton County. There just wasn't a lot of building going on in Henry County back then," Stringer says. "Boy, has that changed."

From five employees in 1972 to sixty five today, from barely $1 million in sales to over $28 million–Lyman Stringer and his employees, through work ethic, attention to detail, and a steadfast commitment to a highly personalized style of service, have built a company that exemplifies the risks and rewards of successful business ownership and development in the United States. "Yeah, we've really worked at it," Stringer states, "and service has always been the key; that's what built the company."

"I bought out my partner in 1982," says Stringer. "We continued to grow along with the County." The company expanded into Butts, Jackson, Fayette, Clayton, Pike, Spaulding and Dekalb Counties, but the phenomenal rate of growth and development in Henry County over the past five years has provided Stringer Lumber with enough homegrown business that working outside the county is now a luxury rather than a necessity. In recent years the company has also diversified from working primarily in the home building industry to a steadily growing involvement with contractors building warehouses and office buildings.

Civic and community involvement has been another trademark of Stringer Lumber Company. The company donates materials for projects and auctions for a number of churches, sports teams and other worthy groups and causes throughout the county.

Doing what is right, regardless of the circumstances–that has been the founding principle of Re/Max Advantage, also known as Southside Partners, since its creation in 1992 by Kent R. Miller, Leslie Edwards, Mike Ward, and Earl Connell. The result of a merger among three separate and individually successful Re/Max offices, the company has dominated the south side of Atlanta as it holds exclusive franchise rights in Clayton, Henry, and Butts Counties and has closed between $20 and $48 million in real estate transactions each month. Re/Max Advantage agents average twenty-four closings per year, while the nearest competitors sell half that amount. The four owners possess over a century of experience in the real estate profession and, between them, have served on the Boards of Realtors and communities in almost every conceivable capacity and logged thousands of educational hours in the field.

To be the undisputed leader in the real estate industry, quality of personnel, market presence, advertising and service to clients is highly valued. Therefore, the company's success has been coupled with over a decade of development and earned it a 2002 sales volume of over $464 million. Growth has remained steady as the firm now includes 150 agents with offices in Stockbridge, Jackson, and Jonesboro. Mike Barry, the fourth partner in the company,

joined Miller, Edwards, and Ward in 2000 and construction of a new building in Jackson was completed in Spring 2001.

Stellar accomplishments such as these are owed in no small part to the service-oriented support that has become a trademark of business at Re/Max Advantage. Their mission statement strongly reflects the reason behind such success in the real estate industry with objectives that will enhance the well-being of Sales Associates by providing ongoing training and encouragement to attain personal and professional goals, strive for a level of excellence in service that surpasses expectations, and become advocates of a fair and honest profit for everyone.

The support of community and charitable activities plays a major role in the lives of Re/Max Advantage partners and agents. Leslie Edwards serves on the board of the Southern Crescent Habitat for Humanity, and agents throughout the company regularly donate percentages of sales commissions to The Children's Miracle Network.

Simply put, Re/Max Advantage offers service and support that is the finest in the real estate industry today. To find out more about the company, its Realtors and broker, locations, and new home listings, please visit www.advantagehousehunt.com.

HARDING PLUMBING AND SUPPLY, INC.

The disastrous effects of a recession on the construction business, the help of a dedicated and talented family, and a steadfast commitment to excellent service and quality products have combined to make Harding Plumbing and Supply, Inc. the industry leader it is today.

William E. (Bill) Harding Sr. was in the construction business when times became tough during the downturn in the mid-seventies. Integrating a plumbing business seemed a good move to take up the slack. He began by primarily doing the plumbing for his own construction, and, in his own words, "having my dinner interrupted by people calling to have a rat removed from their well, or a squirrel from a commode." His wife Frances was his partner in the business from the beginning, and they worked hard to survive the lean times and establish a foothold for the future.

It didn't take long for a couple of builders to express interest in having him do their plumbing. A company with one truck, one employee, and a kitchen table for an office, was on its way to becoming the highly successful and respected enterprise it is today. Harding Plumbing and Supply now has 25 trucks, 34 employees, numerous subcontractors, a half-block-wide storefront, a warehouse, and parking property.

Over the years a number of loyal, hard-working employees have played key roles in the enormous growth and success of the company. Service Manager Kip Adkins and Chief Trouble Shooter Rob "The Magician" Thomas came on board in 1978. Toya Adkins arrived in 1985 and currently manages all seven companies centralized in her office which come under Harding. When Bill was out of the office for several weeks in 1986 due to surgery, Bill and Frances saw that son Jack had the ability and desire to run the day-to-day operations. Jack is now the vice president and general manager of Harding Plumbing. Frances, of course, has always played a critical role in many aspects of the business. She is an owner and the company secretary. In 1992 Dana, Jack's wife joined the team. She changed the office into a computer-friendly operation.

The future for Harding Plumbing and Supply seems bright. Jack and Dana's sons, R. J. and Hudson, who have grown up in the shop, are the third generation in the family business. Whatever the ensuing years bring, the theme of Harding Plumbing will always be "one family doing the best that they can."

At a time when most hospitals are downsizing, Henry Medical Center continues to experience the phenomenal growth that has occurred since the hospital opened its doors on July 9, 1979.

When Henry General Hospital opened it was a small hospital that provided services to a rural county of just thirty-five thousand residents. From the minute the first patient arrived, the hospital experienced unparalleled growth. In 1995 Henry General Hospital was renamed Henry Medical Center to reflect a proactive role to design services in order to meet the future healthcare challenges and to better reflect the comprehensive services being offered. Today, Henry Medical Center is a 124-bed not-for-profit community hospital and admits more than 8,000 patients annually. It offers exceptional medical care to more than 110,000 residents of one of the fastest growing counties in the nation, as well as the residents of adjoining counties.

The medical center is equipped to perform a wide range of medical services. The Emergency Department is one of the busiest departments in the hospital with more than 40,000 patients treated annually. In Labor & Delivery you will find nurses committed to passionate and personal care for new parents and babies and a Neonatal Intensive Care and Newborn Nursery staffed by highly skilled nurses. Physicians and therapists have intensive training in the care of premature and acutely ill newborns. The medical center has the latest technological advances in diagnostic care including nuclear medicine, mammography, x-ray, bone density scanning, upper gastrointestinal series, ultrasound, MRI and CT scanning. The Medical Center recently expanded the Surgery Department where sophisticated surgical procedures that utilize today's newest evolving technology are performed. Other facilities include the Cardiac Catheterization Lab that offers the latest technology for monitoring and diagnosing the condition of the heart; the newly built Laurel Park, a skilled nursing and rehabilitation facility, that adds to the hospital's continuum of care; and a Community Education program that reaches out to more than forty thousand residents of Henry County every year.

The heart of Henry Medical Center's vision is superior people providing superior healthcare services. The hospital values its role as a premier resource to enhance the quality of life in Henry County and to provide the best in healthcare services.

Above: Henry Medical Center, 2002.

Below: A caring community of health professionals stands ready to provide outstanding care to even the smallest of patients.

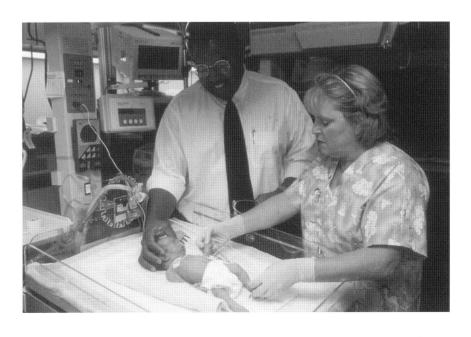

ELESYS NORTH AMERICA INC.

FORMERLY

NEC

TECHNOLOGIES

A Global Fortune 500 company with more than 130,000 employees worldwide and $43 billion in revenues, NEC has a history of more than one hundred years of leadership and innovation in high technology. The company has become a trusted leader in technology solutions that will meet the explosive growth and demand occurring in the field today.

This global company maintains a worldwide network of consolidated subsidiaries, manufacturing plants, marketing, service, research and development firms and liaison offices that provide integral technologies.

The McDonough plant operation of NEC was established in July 1985. Cherry blossom trees planted in honor of significant company events, friends, visitors, and lost loved ones greet visitors. NEC was one of Henry County's largest employers, with over six hundred employees. The company occupied two manufacturing buildings and one distribution center. Products manufactured included televisions, projection TVs, laptop computers, computer monitors, automotive electronics, as well as CD-ROM and printer refurbishment. Though the operation is now much smaller, the desire and ability to continue to provide quality, technologically advanced products has not diminished. The McDonough facility has now shifted its talent to research and development of automotive safety products, such as the SeatSentry™ occupant sensing systems and airbag control modules.

Throughout the years, employees of NEC have long believed in supporting their community and have achieved a stellar reputation among local and national organizations. Money, items, and even blood have been collected and donated to such worthy charitable causes as the March of Dimes, Red Cross, United Way, Battered Women's Shelter, the Angel on a Tree program, the Counsel on Aging, and the Sheriff's Youth Homes. Computers and monitors have been donated to local schools and other organizations in Henry County, as well. Successful recycling programs have also rewarded employees with tennis and basketball court and a walking track.

Founded well over thirty-five years ago and accredited by the U.S. Chamber of Commerce, the Henry County Chamber of Commerce is a private, nonprofit corporation that unites businesses and professional firms who are committed to progress in all of Henry County. The Chamber promotes future business growth, provides support for existing businesses and industry, works to improve the current business environment and strives to help provide superior education and overall quality of life for the citizens of Henry County.

The eight hundred Chamber of Commerce members do more than own and operate businesses here. They live, raise families, send children to school, shop, take walks in the parks, serve in the government and the school board, and volunteer for civic and community organizations. Solid businesses are vital to the health of a community, providing a tax base for government services, jobs for our youth, and goods and services for everyone. The Chamber makes it its business to promote good businesses and good business practices in the county.

Chamber activities, committees and programs promote business and encourage interaction between members and non-members to make things happen. The Chamber sponsors activities, committees and programs, including the Annual Trade Show; Business Before Hours; Business Boosters Luncheon; Business After Hours; Business Ambassadors; Education Committee; Government Affairs Committee; Small Business Council; Cultural Development Committee; Media Relations Committee; Transportation Committee; Existing Industries Council; Keep Henry Clean and Beautiful; Membership Development Committee; Leadership Henry; Youth Leadership Henry; Student Teacher Achievement Breakfast; New Teacher Induction Program; Leadership Appreciation Dinner; Annual Golf Classic; Annual Meeting/Banquet; and New Member Reception.

The Chamber's national award-winning website, www.henrycounty.com, receives over thirty thousand hits monthly. *Visions*, the Chamber's monthly publication, reaches 6,000 citizens, and their networking events and informational meetings serve over 3,000 members and non-members annually.

In addition to the Chamber of Commerce, there are two other organizations that work together to foster growth and progress in the county, the Henry County Convention and Visitors Bureau and the Henry County Development Authority. The Visitor Bureau is an extension of the Chamber and exists to promote Henry County as a visitor destination or stop over point. It participates in group-tour and travel trade shows and responds to thousands of requests for information annually. The Henry County Development Authority exists to promote new and current industry expansion. The Authority is responsible for, but not limited to, attracting new industrial and commercial prospects; promoting development of industrial parks and freestanding industrial sites for use by expanding and new businesses; and maintaining legislative liaison with local, state, and national legislative delegations.

Above: The Henry County Chamber of Commerce can be reached at 1709 Highway 20 West, Westridge Business Center, McDonough, Georgia 30253; by phone at 770-957-5786; by email at memberservices@henrycounty.com; or at www.henrycounty.com

Below: The Hudgins Room, the Chamber's community room, offers seating capacity up to 125, a full caterer's kitchen and an inviting courtyard.

BARRY HURST & ASSOCIATES REALTY

✧

Above: Barry Hurst, broker/owner.

Below: Barry Hurst & Associates Reality, a world of service.

One of the most recognized and well-respected leaders in the industry today, Broker/Owner Barry Hurst has maintained a remarkable career in real estate that has spanned over a decade and encompassed a wide range of accomplishments and service-oriented professionalism in the field. His company, Barry Hurst & Associates Realty, daily applies the motto "A World of Service" as they build lasting relationships and positive results for local and international customers and clients—and that is what sets Barry Hurst & Associates Realty apart from others in the business. Barry and his outstanding team of agents and staff are characterized by a focus and determination that reflects their desire to successfully help people realize a rewarding home sale or to purchase a dream home.

After receiving his real estate license in 1987, his natural ability and intense desire to offer quality service in every transaction offered Hurst a number of exciting opportunities and rewards in the business. In 1996 the Metro South Association of Realtors, grossing over $19 million in one year, named him real estate agent of the year. He has received numerous honors including a lifetime achievement award by ReMax International and has spent sixteen consecutive years in the Million-Dollar Club. He was awarded the Zenith Award and Gold Award from the Metro South Board of Realtors, and is consistently recognized as one of Atlanta's "Top 100 Residential Realtors." He has been a featured speaker on a Top Producers Panel for the Howard Brinton Seminars where he addressed thousands of realtors from across the country, and is included in the esteemed *Atlanta Business Chronicle* for his outstanding achievements.

When Barry Hurst ventured out on his own in 2001 to form Barry Hurst & Associates Realty, he was joined by a dedicated and well-qualified team including co-owner and office manager, Judy Stubblefield, five agents and a number of staff members. Headquartered at 1625 Highway 42 North in McDonough, over three thousand customers are included in the company's database of residential, commercial, and land sale activities.

Barry remains dedicated to his volunteer and charitable work in the community and sponsors a number of organizations including several local ball teams, the Georgia Brain Tumor Foundation, American Cancer Society, Rainbow House, Habitat for Humanity, and Southwest Christian Hospice.

For more information, please visit Barry Hurst & Associates Realty on the Internet at www.barryhurstandassociates.com, or by call 770-914-2306.

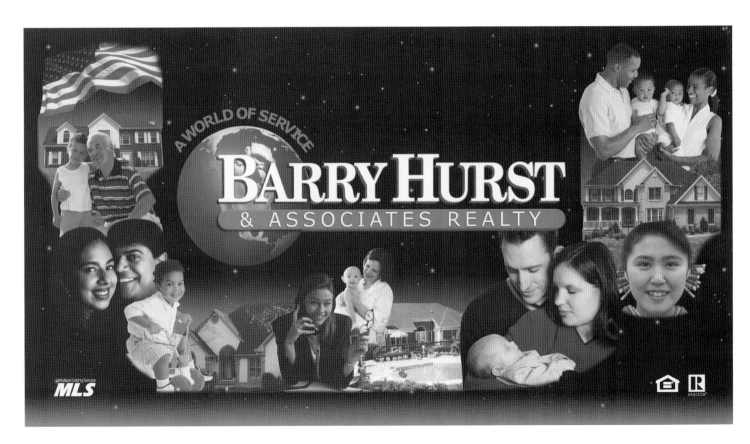

Comfort and quality are only a reservation away at AmeriHost Inn, the AAA Three Diamond rated hotel located at 100 North Park Court in Stockbridge.

The AmeriHost Inn is a multi-story building with interior guest room access. The hotel's guest rooms offer electronic door locks, in-room coffee, safes, hairdryers, irons and ironing boards, and data-ports, to mention a few of our convenient in-room amenities. A signature element of the building is the beautiful indoor pool and whirlpool area located off the lobby of the hotel. Whirlpool suites feature in-room whirlpools, microfridges, and expanded seating areas. The executive suites offer balconies overlooking the indoor pool. Other amenities include express checkout, expanded complimentary continental breakfast, free USA Today newspapers, a meeting room, an exercise area, and twenty-five-inch color television with remote control and in-room movies on demand for all registered guests.

Convenient location also provides easy access to several major area attractions. The excitement of an Atlanta Falcons football game in the Georgia Dome or the thrill of an Atlanta Hawks basketball game in the Omni Coliseum remains a popular event throughout the year. Major League Baseball is alive and well as the Atlanta Braves play in Turner Olympic Stadium. Avid golfers will also appreciate the choice of several award-winning courses nearby—Green Valley Golf Club, Cotton Fields Golf Club, and Eagles Landing Country Club. The Tanger Outlet Mall and Peachtree Peddlers Flea Market provide visitors countless hours of shopping and entertainment for the whole family. And for anyone needing quick access to Henry General Hospital, AmeriHost Inn is only a half-mile away. Popular local eateries include Outback Steakhouse, Buckhead Brewery, Affairs by Pinehurst Tea Room & Catering, Buffalo's Cafe, Cafe Chavez, Captain Billy's Fish House, Chaser's Bar & Grill, and Cherdan's Seafood Restaurant.

AMERIHOST INN

LEGACY FORD-MERCURY

So how does one take a bankrupt, closed automobile dealership and turn it into the centerpiece of a $100-million enterprise, the third largest minority-owned business in the Greater Atlanta area in just ten years? Education, preparation, vision, dedication—these are all traits that allowed Emanuel Jones to author Legacy Ford-Mercury's remarkable story.

An Atlanta native, Emanuel Davie Jones was the valedictorian of his 1977 West Fulton High School graduating class, won an academic scholarship to the University of Pennsylvania, where he was a member of both the varsity track and football teams, and graduated with honors in electrical engineering. He rose to the rank of Captain in the United States Army Corps of Engineers and accepted a position with IBM as a product engineer. He was granted an academic leave of absence and received his MBA in Finance and Accounting from Columbia University in 1986. After a stint with Arthur Anderson as a management consultant, Jones was accepted into Ford Motor Company's Dealer Training Program.

In October 1991 Jones was offered an opportunity that was laden with both opportunity and high risk. He accepted the challenge of reviving a closed Ford dealership in McDonough. His wife Gloria told him, "Emanuel, you are coming back to your home, your roots and your beginning." Her words were the inspiration for the name of the dealership—Legacy Ford-Mercury, Inc., and the company's theme—"Come Back to Your Legacy."

Legacy Ford-Mercury has grown from 12 employees to over 250 employees. Jones has added Legacy Toyota in Union City; Legendary Ford-Mercury in Marion, North Carolina; a Goodyear franchise in McDonough; and an ANSA Automotive in McDonough to his growing list of enterprises

The vision statement of Legacy Ford, Inc., reflects Jones' steadfast belief in the crucial role of exemplary service to the company's success. Our vision is to provide a great work environment for our employees, which will create an exceptional sales and service experience for our customer; an experience so good that they will want to tell their friends and neighbors about the dealership's superior quality, friendly atmosphere, and excellent reputation.

Is there one key lesson Jones has learned from the meteoric rise of Legacy Ford and his other successful ventures? He states, "Never invest your money in a business venture if you're not willing to invest your heart and soul first, your time and mind second."

❖

Emanuel Davie Jones.

Harry Norman, REALTORS® is one of the most widely known and well-respected real estate companies in Georgia. Headquartered in Atlanta and licensed in Georgia and North Carolina, their agents are located in numerous regions across greater Atlanta including Towne Lake, Cobb North, North Fulton, Medlock Bridge, Country Club of the South, East Cobb, Cobb/Marietta, Buckhead/Sandy Springs, Buckhead/Northwest, Gwinnett/DeKalb, Buckhead at Powers Ferry, Intown and Dunwoody/Perimeter. The company also maintains offices outside of Atlanta in McDonough, Peachtree City, Mall of Georgia, North Georgia and in the city of Highlands, North Carolina.

Harry Norman, REALTORS® was the first exclusively residential firm in Atlanta and was founded in 1930 to provide customers with outstanding service and professionalism in the sale or purchase of a home. Today, the company is proud to be Greater Atlanta's largest independent real estate firm. Helping customers carefully and quickly buy or sell a home, no matter what the price range, has been the single most important factor in the great success Harry Norman, REALTORS® has sustained over the last seven decades.

Whether customers are buying, selling, relocating or financing the home of their dreams, Harry Norman, REALTORS® stands ready to guide them with highly qualified agents who have the training and motivation to make customers' dreams come true. Knowledge of local home values, pricing and negotiations are all important assets in getting the most for a home. Award-winning relocation packages and information and resources on topics ranging from education and healthcare to housing and area attractions continue to help customers make well-educated decisions in moving to the Atlanta area.

The McDonough office of Harry Norman, REALTORS® is directed by owner/broker Kris Cawley and includes over thirty of the finest and most qualified real estate agents in the business today. Their offices are located at 70 Macon Street while agents and their full listing of homes can be accessed through the company's website at www.harrynorman.com.

HARRY NORMAN, REALTORS®

ROBINSON, WHALEY, HAMMONDS & ALLISON, P.C. CERTIFIED PUBLIC ACCOUNTANTS & CONSULTANTS

Above: Lewis Robinson, founder of Robinson, Whaley, Hammonds & Allison, P.C.

Below: The offices of Robinson, Whaley, Hammonds & Allison, P.C. at 1200 Keys Ferry Court in McDonough, Georgia.

The firm of Robinson, Whaley, Hammonds & Allison P.C. has served metropolitan Atlanta's Southern Crescent area since 1991, dedicating itself to families and businesses in need of the highest level of professional advice. Their extensive accounting, tax and estate planning experience enables them to personally and innovatively serve their clients in dealing with financial concerns.

Lewis Robinson founded the firm in September of 1991 after many years of owning or managing several successful businesses in the Southern Crescent. His practice focuses on business and estate consulting as well as tax planning during life changing situations.

Patty Whaley joined the firm shortly after its inception. She brings extensive experience in accounting technology and provides expertise in both the installation of and training on computer software.

Greg Hammonds has been RWH&A since 1995 after more than a decade with an Atlanta firm. His practice focuses on income taxation with a particular emphasis in the areas of estates and trusts.

In 1998, Alvin Allison became a member of the firm, joining it after many years in practice with other firms. He specializes in consulting and tax planning for small businesses and individual clients. He also oversees the firm's review and compilation engagements.

In addition to traditional accounting and tax services, the firm has recently created

two new companies. Qualified Intermediary Services LLC provides assistance in completing tax-deferred property exchanges. PayAccurate LLC provides payroll services to its clients.

For more information, visit the firm's website at www.rwhcpa.com. As you browse through the site, you will see highlighted background information on the firm and the services it provides, as well as many useful resources such as informative articles and interactive financial calculators. In addition, the firm has taken the time to gather many links to external websites that would be of interest to its clients and visitors.

Please feel free to contact the firm with any questions or comments you may have. The members of the firm pride themselves on being responsive to clients' inquiries and suggestions.

The clear and prophetic vision of Michael and Sharon Singley led to the opening in March 1995 of one of Henry County's most respected and successful professional offices. Deeply involved in the optical business for over twenty years, they realized a need in the Locust Grove area for a full-service vision center. The Eye Center of Locust Grove fills that need.

Dennis Matzkin, M.D., and George Courtright, M.D., were instrumental in the success of the Eye Center, and assisted in establishing the foundation and policies that allowed the enterprise to grow rapidly. A health fair in the town of McDonough, at which the Eye Center promoted its motto that "your eyes are the windows to your body," also had a major impact on the Singley's new business. One of the Center's optometrists likely saved a woman's vision with his perceptive diagnosis.

For many years, the Eye Center of Locust Grove was located in the old downtown historical section of Locust Grove. It is now located at the south end of the new Ingles Shopping Center for greater convenience for customers. They have added a surgery room to perform lasik and cataract surgeries on site.

EYE CENTER OF LOCUST GROVE

The Eye Center offers a wide selection of frames, lenses, contact lenses, Lasik and Cataract surgery by Dr. Dennis Matzkin and treatment of various diseases of the eye. Three O.D.'s, two M.D.'s, and two licensed opticians are on the staff. With over five thousand customers in the greater Henry County area, a close relationship with businesses such as Snapper Power and Equipment, and the transition of Henry County to a healthcare provider, The Eye Center of Locust Grove has every reason to expect its dramatic growth and success to continue.

❖
The comfortable waiting area at The Eye Center of Locust Grove.

A strong tradition of unwavering dedication to the highest quality in Chiropractic care runs deep in the family of Dr. Keith Crowe. When he opened Crowe Chiropractic, P.C. in March of 2000, Dr. Crowe was assuring the lofty standards of his father's forty-eight-year-old College Park practice would be carried on in the Eagle's Landing area in Henry County.

Key individuals during the development and growth of Crowe Chiropractic were Dr. Crowe's wife Lorna, his mother Elizabeth, and, of course, his father. His brother, Dr. Hal S. Crowe, a noted Chiropractor in Brunswick, Georgia, also provided his expertise. Crowe Chiropractic, P.C. employs two doctors and three staff members.

The mission of Crowe Chiropractic is to help improve and maintain health through Chiropractic to all who seek it; keeping the spinal vertebrae free of subluxation, and allowing free flow of mental impulse between brain and body, body and brain. Crowe

CROWE CHIROPRACTIC, P.C.

Chiropractic strives to foster and promote knowledge of drug-free healing, knowing that healing comes from within and that health is not merely the absence of infirmary.

❖
Dr. Keith Crowe.

RoLanka International, Inc.

"Sustainable vegetation offers a far more environmentally friendly approach for control of soil erosion than concrete or other hard armor methods," according to Calista Santha, Ph.D., co-owner of RoLanka International. "Our goal is to educate the public and the construction industry to the critical dangers of sediment pollution and the enormous benefits of ecologically-sound approaches and products to control these problems."

RoLanka International, Inc., founded in 1993 by the husband and wife team of B. Lanka Santha, P. E., and Calista Santha, Ph.D., is one of the very few Henry County erosion and sedimentation control companies that concentrate on environmentally friendly systems and products. Coir, a natural by-product of coconut fiber, is the base for most of the RoLanka product line.

"It doesn't make sense to attempt to restore the environment to a healthy state by utilizing methods that will harm it," states Calista. "The staggering increase in development, population, and the resulting soil erosion and water pollution in our local area is a microcosm of the staggering

environmental problems from soil erosion facing the world at large. Any time dirt is disturbed by construction and the soil left exposed, sediments harmful to water supplies, and thus harmful to life, have a high probability of draining into those water supplies. RoLanka is committed to stemming and reversing the harmful effects of this erosion."

Bruster's Ice Cream

❖

Left: David "Rocky" Smith.

Center: Paul and Betty Smith with their family.

Right: Sondra Smith.

Enjoying the "country life" was the motivating factor that caused entrepreneurs Paul and Betty Smith to move to McDonough in Henry County in 1973. And along with their children and grandchildren, they have enjoyed their fifteen acres on Campground Road.

But along the way the couple became leaders in business, community, and church affairs. They own Smith Electric Contracting, a forty-year success story, operated Precious Memories Antiques on the square in McDonough for nine years, and own and operate Bruster's Ice Cream, located on Highway 155 near 1-75.

Through all the business and time commitments of this remarkable couple, they have always placed their family first. And quite a family it is. Sondra,

Paul, Jr., David, Joseph, Matthew, and Joshua are their six children, and along with daughters-in-law Tonya, Tammy, Heather, and Amy, they have presented Paul and Betty with nine grandchildren. Paul III, Jacob, Toni, Benjamin, Kala, Chelsee, David II, Patrick, and Harrison all reside in Henry County.

Bruster's is a favorite gathering place for members of First Baptist Church and Salem Baptist, as well as other members of the community.

The land that the City of McDonough now occupies was once the home of a tribe of the Creek Indians. It now holds a bustling community of thousands and is the county seat of one of the fastest growing counties in the country.

Fertile soil and plentiful game that attracted and kept the Creek Indians in the area during the latter stages of the Civil War, was referred to as the "Egypt of the Confederacy." It was the great granary that fed the armies still in the field,

when the resources of almost every other part of the South had been exhausted.

The Civil War and McDonough were tightly intertwined. Sherman sent Kilpatrick's "raiders" to scout the town as he moved on Atlanta, and after the city fell apart of the massive Federal Army moving south occupied McDonough for enough hours to cause serious damage, although the city was spared the destructive torch so many others suffered.

Founded in the early 1820s, McDonough was named for Commodore Thomas McDonough. The city has grown steadily over the years, but has seen an explosive spurt over the past decade. A thriving business community, a true sense of neighborhood and community, and its proximity to the City of Atlanta, the world's busiest airport, and numerous attractions and events are a powerful draw. Atlanta Motor Speedway, Turner Field (home of the Atlanta Braves), Georgia National Golf Club–are all within a few minutes of the city center of McDonough.

CITY OF MCDONOUGH

Henry County Courthouse built in 1897 with the tower, bell and clock. Here you will find records dating back to the early 1800s.

A start-up business in the home, the closing of a foreign bank, and naps between jobs in parking lots, are a few of the dynamics that have led to the dramatic growth of one of Henry County's most successful young businesses.

J. Bentley Rainwater is an independent fee appraiser who has been serving the Atlanta area

since 1993, founded the Rainwater Group Appraisal Services, L.L.P. when he was employed at Rockwell International. When the Japanese Bank that employed Bentley's wife Sandy closed its doors, she brought her considerable marketing, bookkeeping and office management skills to the company. The Rainwater Group's growth was so rapid that at one time there were eight employees and computers, three printers, a fax machine, and three cocker spaniels in the Rainwater's bonus room.

The Rainwater Group Appraisal Services is firmly committed to increasing the industry standard by providing the highest quality residential property appraisal reports, in the timeliest fashion, through a sincere dedication to customer service.

Rainwater has doubled in size. Their volume of the business has also doubled each year since 1998, and there are plans to build their own office building in the not too distant future.

The company is very active in supporting local youth sports, youth church activities and schools.

RAINWATER GROUP APPRAISAL SERVICES

J. Bentley Rainwater, owner of Rainwater Group Appraisal Services.

FIRST BAPTIST CHURCH OF STOCKBRIDGE

✧

First Baptist Church of Stockbridge is located at 4566 North Henry Boulevard in Stockbridge, Georgia.

First Baptist Church of Stockbridge was founded September 1, 1917 with 18 members and has now grown to 839 members. First Baptist Church is a member of the Henry Association of Baptist Churches, the Georgia Baptist Convention and the Southern Baptist Convention.

First Baptist Church has helped to establish Ellenwood First Baptist, Jodeco Baptist, and North Henry Baptist Churches. Ministries now include children, student, choir, and orchestra; an academy for K-5; mission trips expanding to include global ministry; ministry to homeless, womens, and children shelters, and a local care pregnancy center; support of local YMCA, local Cub Scout troops, and much more.

In 2003, a new worship center was added to seat about a thousand people. First Baptist Church of Stockbridge is committed to reaching out to the community and exalting God's greatness.

APPLE REALTY, INC.

In 1974 a small real estate agency began with two licensed agents whose goal was to build a reputation by offering the best service possible for each of its clients. This goal was quickly met as the demand for such exceptional personal service in the real estate business grew.

The company kept pace with the growth by adding highly qualified professional real estate agents to its team. In 1991 the company incorporated as Apple Realty, Inc. Today, headquartered in a 6,000-square-foot office, the agency has over thirty real estate professionals who uphold the tradition of unparalleled service in the real estate community.

Based in Stockbridge, Apple provides service to all metro Atlanta counties and offers a wide range of real estate services from new home sales to resales to commercial sales. A recipient of the Henry County "Small Business of the Year" award, Apple Realty, Inc. recognizes its responsibility to the community. Among other activities, it sponsors youth sports teams and a program to furnish computers to students in local schools.

In 1980 Harold "Hal" C. Johnson, Jr. founded Peach State Carpet in Decatur, Georgia at the corner of Covington Highway and Redan Road. Thomas B. Johnson, Sr. and Robert "Bob" A. Johnson joined the expanding business a short while later. The trio disbanded in 1985 as Hal bought Godfather Customs and Bob began developing and building homes. Thomas became sole owner and president of Peach State Carpet that year and, with construction at an all-time high in the area, relocated the company to Stockbridge and the bustling community of Henry County in 1986.

Today, Peach State Carpet offers all types of carpet, hardwood flooring, ceramic tile, vinyl flooring, and window treatments. Community activities remain a high priority for the company as they support local football, baseball, and soccer teams, as well as marching bands and cheerleading squads in Stockbridge, Union Grove, Eagles Landing, and McDonough. Peach State Carpet is also a strong supporter of the annual Shriners Hospital Crusade.

For all your flooring needs, come by and visit the friendly staff at Peach State Carpet at 4062 North Henry Boulevard in Stockbridge.

PEACH STATE CARPET

SPONSORS

For more information about the following publications, please call 800-749-0464 or visit www.lammertinc.com.

Historic Abilene: An Illustrated History
Historic Amarillo: An Illustrated History
Historic Anchorage: An Illustrated History
Historic Austin: An Illustrated History
Historic Beaumont: An Illustrated History
Historic Brazoria County: An Illustrated History
Historic Cape Girardeau: An Illustrated History
Historic Charlotte: An Illustrated History of Charlotte and Mecklenburg County
Historic Corpus Christi: An Illustrated History
Historic Denton County: An Illustrated History
Historic Edmond: An Illustrated History
Historic El Paso: An Illustrated History
Historic Erie County: An Illustrated History
Historic Fairbanks: An Illustrated History
Historic Gainesville & Hall County: An Illustrated History
Historic Houston: An Illustrated History
Historic Kern County: An Illustrated History of Bakersfield and Kern County
Historic Laredo: An Illustrated History of Laredo & Webb County
Historic Louisiana: An Illustrated History
Historic Midland: An Illustrated History
Historic Montgomery County: An Illustrated History of Montgomery County, Texas
Historic Oklahoma: An Illustrated History
Historic Oklahoma County: An Illustrated History
Historic Omaha: An Illustrated History of Omaha and Douglas County
Historic Pasadena: An Illustrated History
Historic Passaic County: An Illustrated History
Historic Philadelphia: An Illustrated History
Historic Richardson: An Illustrated History
Historic Rio Grande Valley: An Illustrated History
Historic Scottsdale: A Life from the Land
Historic Shreveport-Bossier: An Illustrated History of Shreveport & Bossier City
Historic Texas: An Illustrated History
Historic Tulare County: A Sesquicentennial History, 1852-2002
Historic Victoria: An Illustrated History
Historic Williamson County: An Illustrated History
Iron, Wood & Water: An Illustrated History of Lake Oswego
Miami's Historic Neighborhoods: A History of Community
Old Orange County Courthouse: A Centennial History
Plano: An Illustrated Chronicle